NO SAFE SPACES

DENNIS MARK
PRAGER JOSEPH

EDITORS

NO
SAFE
SPACES

with a foreword by ADAM CAROLLA

REGNERY PUBLISHING

A Division of Salem Media Group

Regnery® is a registered trademark of Salem Communications Holding Corporation

Cataloging-in-Publication data on file with the Library of Congress

ISBN 978-1-62157-865-9
ebook ISBN 978-1-62157-982-3

Published in the United States by
Regnery Publishing
A Division of Salem Media Group
300 New Jersey Ave NW
Washington, DC 20001
www.Regnery.com

Manufactured in the United States of America

10 9 8 7 6 5 4 3 2 1

Books are available in quantity for promotional or premium use. For information on discounts and terms, please visit our website: www.Regnery.com.

CONTENTS

Foreword by Adam Carolla   vii

CHAPTER ONE
Showing Up for Work Is the New Racism   1

CHAPTER TWO
Safe Spaces versus Free Speech   15

CHAPTER THREE
White Privilege and the Culture of Victimhood   33

CHAPTER FOUR
In Which We Mansplain Feminism and Gender Politics   53

CHAPTER FIVE
Leftism, Liberalism, and Language   69

CHAPTER SIX
Academic Failure   85

CHAPTER SEVEN
Unsafe Spaces   107

CHAPTER EIGHT
Where Are the Adults?   121

CHAPTER NINE
Losing the American Trinity   135

CHAPTER TEN
Political Correctness Moves Off-Campus 145

CHAPTER ELEVEN
That's Not Funny! PC Kills Art 157

CHAPTER TWELVE
Poisoning Our Politics 175

CHAPTER THIRTEEN
What Can Parents Do? 193

CHAPTER FOURTEEN
How Educators Can Do Better 213

CHAPTER FIFTEEN
Get Happy (or, This Is All Your Responsibility) 231

EPILOGUE
Reason for Hope 245

Notes 253
Index 257

FOREWORD

BY ADAM CAROLLA

I grew up in North Hollywood, California. Sounds glamourous, right? Well, if the Hollywood you're picturing is celebrities at a white-tablecloth five-star restaurant with seven different forks, North Hollywood is a diner where the waitresses blow smoke rings while pouring your coffee.

Growing up on food stamps and welfare, I (barely) graduated high school and went right to work in construction. Let me be clear: this was not the "construction" you see in TV ads with well-groomed white guys in hardhats looking at blueprints. I did manual labor—digging ditches, cleaning up garbage, and other work fit for a donkey. I worked hard, paid attention and listened to the guys with experience, and learned the trade of carpenter. (Just like Jesus!)

Construction is lonely work, and often my only company was a radio, tuned to—you guessed it—*The Dennis Prager Show*. It never occurred to me that someday I would be on Dennis's show, where he would be interviewing…*me*. But it happened in 2011, and it became immediately clear that despite very different paths in life, we shared important values. I've often said that the thing Dennis and I have in common is common sense.

We believe in individualism: that by taking responsibility for our fates, we make our own success. For Dennis, that meant going off the beaten path in high school and college. For me, it meant launching my own radio show without a radio station.

We both spend hours each week interviewing interesting people, and, like any good talk junkie, we crave open, interesting discussion. We both need that hit every day. That authenticity is critical if you want to engage with and understand the world. My parents were checked-out messes who played victim like Eric Clapton plays guitar. So I respect anyone with the intellectual honesty to assert and also challenge his own beliefs. Since way back in 2011, at the time of my first interview on his show, Dennis and I haven't seen nearly enough of that type of ego-checking happening in America. In fact, even then the concept of free thought was under attack in the very place it should have been thriving: academia. (Wow, "Academia"—pretty big word for a guy who barely graduated high school.)

So it seemed only natural that Dennis and I would go into the belly of the beast and start speaking on college campuses, warning parents, students, and faculty about the dangers of shutting down free speech that was deemed politically incorrect or provocative.

Ironically (as you're about to read) they promptly proved us right.

The good news is, there are other ways to reach a large audience with an important message. That's why we teamed up with producer Mark Joseph to create a movie called *No Safe Spaces*. And that's why the two of them decided to publish this book by the same name.

What follows is a sometimes funny, often disturbing, but always insightful look at a real problem facing America today. Mark and Dennis do a superb job recounting (and expounding on) the horror stories we encountered on campuses across the nation. Along the way, you'll meet some of America's top experts on free speech. And you may even glean some insights and observations from the Ace Man.

If you're interested in defending the liberal tradition of free speech—or even if you're just curious about why a Jewish intellectual (Dennis), the son of missionaries (Mark), and an atheist from Hollywood (moi—that's Mexican for me) would team up to take on Big Academia—then read on!

CHAPTER ONE

SHOWING UP FOR WORK IS THE NEW RACISM

Professor Bret Weinstein couldn't believe his own eyes.

Were people spying on him?

As Weinstein, an Evergreen State College biology professor who considers himself "deeply progressive," biked into town from his house that early spring morning in 2017, he could have sworn he saw students from the school eyeing him suspiciously as he pedaled by. What were they doing in his neighborhood?

The professor had good reason to be on edge. He had found himself at the center of a heated—and very one-sided—discussion about race at this very progressive liberal arts college, located in Olympia, Washington.

It hadn't gone well.

What started as a public meeting chaired by the college president soon devolved into a protest in which Weinstein was shouted at and shouted down.

That morning, for the second day in a row, the campus police had told him it would be better if he didn't show up on campus. If he wasn't around, maybe things would cool off a bit.

But Weinstein had a biology class to teach, so he arranged to meet his students at a park downtown, off school property. That Thursday morning, May 2017, he tucked his crop of unruly black hair into a bike helmet and pedaled his way into town, looking every bit the stereotypical liberal college professor straight out of central casting. He could not have looked more the part if he had been wearing a beret.

But through the rural, tree-lined roads near his house he noticed something weird.

"I saw people that I recognized from the protest the day before," Weinstein said. As he biked past them, Weinstein thought he saw them taking out their phones, as if they were sending messages.

Was he really being tailed by student protesters? It sure seemed like it. Unsettled, Weinstein went to Evergreen after all—right to the campus police department. He told them what he had seen—though he realized how kooky he must sound.

"I must be imagining it," Weinstein concluded.

The police disagreed. They told Weinstein the protesters had been looking for him. Worse still, the police told Professor Bret Weinstein that they couldn't protect him.

What crime had this monster, Bret Weinstein, committed to enrage a group of Evergreen State College students?

He showed up to work.

⊘

When you think of people needing protection, you may think of a former mafioso going into a witness protection program. But Evergreen's Vito Corleone was a Birkenstock-clad interdisciplinary studies major who is convinced the only reason we all aren't wearing hemp shirts is the aftereffects of nineteenth-century British mercantilism.

Before 2017, Evergreen State College might have been best known as the alma mater of rapper Macklemore and Matt Groening, creator of *The Simpsons.* The school's motto (and we're not making this up) is *Omnia Extares,* which translates to "Let it all hang out." Its mission statement reads like an academic buzzword bingo card, boasting a "local and global commitment to social justice, diversity, environmental stewardship and service in the public interest." Bernie Sanders couldn't have said it better.

One expression of Evergreen's commitment to diversity was an annual tradition called the "National Day of Absence." This event entails minority faculty and students' leaving campus for a day to make a statement, followed by a day of reunification when everyone appreciates everyone else a bit more or sings "Kumbaya." It's probably not the most effective use of two days of higher learning, but it sounds pretty harmless, right?

It was. Until 2017, when Evergreen wanted to change things up. Instead of minority students and faculty leaving campus for the day, they would show up. *White* students and faculty would stay away. When he heard the plan announced in a faculty meeting, Weinstein "assumed I had misunderstood what had been said." But he soon found there was no mistake. "The administration of the college made it clear that they were strongly encouraging white people not to come to school on that day."

Weinstein found that hard to stomach. "This was people organizing this protest telling others not to show up to a public college on a particular day because of the color of their skin," he noted.

In an e-mail to the all-faculty listserv, he promised to be on campus teaching that day.

On the "Day of Absence" Bret Weinstein biked to campus, as was his routine. The first sign that something was amiss came during his first class; an anxious former student flagged him down to tell him that a mob of students outside the building was chanting for him to be fired.

When Weinstein tried to engage the protesters, he faced a wall of accusations about racial insensitivity. He tried to reply but found he couldn't finish a sentence. Finally, exasperated, he blurted, "Would you like to hear the answer or not?" Several students shouted, "No!"—and kept on haranguing him.

Demonstrations on racial issues—in some cases, targeting Weinstein—continued in the coming weeks. As the protesters grew louder and more aggressive, Evergreen administrators seemed only more eager to appease them in hopes that the problem would just go away. But this only lent the movement legitimacy, which in turn emboldened more extreme behavior—a giant snowball of crazy rolling down a mountain faster and faster, getting bigger and gaining momentum. In late May 2017 demonstrators occupied Evergreen's administration building, storming in and chanting, "Hey, hey, ho, ho, racist teachers got to go." College president George Bridges agreed to a public meeting to discuss the issues. Weinstein figured he should show up to address any allegations lodged against him. (Let's not forget what Weinstein's sin was: daring to show up for work on a work day.)

Whatever illusions Weinstein may have had about the meeting being a civil, open public forum to discuss important issues went down the tubes early on. Before the public meeting started, student organizers admonished any white participants to give up chairs to minority students. Another announcement told white participants to leave water and refreshments alone—like the chairs, those were reserved for minority students.

Once organizers had finished telling people what they could do and where they could go based on their skin color, they were finally ready to address the school's racial issues.

Sure enough, the open forum quickly descended into another excuse for students to yell at Weinstein. This time, the president of the college—the guy who was supposed to be in charge—was there in the room, and he showed no evidence that he was willing or able to do anything to stop it. A text from a former student tipped Weinstein off that some of the protesters would try to stop him from leaving the room. They let him leave, but when a female student tried to engage Weinstein and ask him questions, other protesters berated her and later forced her to read an apology letter at a public rally.

The morning after the protests, Weinstein received a call from Evergreen State College Police Chief Stacy Brown.

"Don't come to campus," Brown warned him. "Protesters are hunting for someone car-to-car, and we think it's you." She said that students had set up impromptu checkpoints at campus entrances and were searching incoming vehicles. President Bridges had ordered Brown and her police department not to interfere.

The morning after being warned by the school's police chief, Weinstein took his bike ride into town, only to see protesters posted along his typical commute route, eagerly tapping at their phones as he pedaled by. The protestors continued watching him as he beelined for the Evergreen State College police department...only to be told that the campus police could do nothing for him.

"You're not safe on campus, and you're not safe anywhere in town on your bicycle," they told him.

"Evergreen is describing a future that is rapidly approaching," Weinstein now warns. He and his wife, fellow biology professor Heather Heying, have both left the school. While Weinstein freely admits that what happened to him was an extreme case, you can look at other college campuses and see the trend in the direction of an illiberal mob mentality.

The whole point of college used to be expanding the mind. Academia gave you the opportunity to think about things in brand-new ways. And yet today, walk onto many of America's most prestigious university campuses, and you'll find a culture that is the complete antithesis of open-minded intellectual inquiry.

Identity politics and political correctness have taken over. Leftist mobs are enforcing a strict code that defines acceptable speech and thought, and rules anything else out of bounds. "Trigger warnings" and "safe spaces" shield students from any concepts that might upset this delicate construct. Dissenters from the new orthodoxy are ostracized, vilified, threatened, and even physically attacked. Opposing viewpoints are shut down; visiting speakers are shut out. Faculty and administrators, whose job it is to help enlighten younger minds, act as hapless enablers, giving free rein to student activists whose passion outreaches their emotional maturity.

The values that supposedly define academia—the pursuit of knowledge and the open exchange of ideas—have become sad casualties. Free thought is not allowed if it broaches concepts deemed "problematic." When you enroll at a college or university today, you can expect four years of being told what to think—and precious few opportunities for critical thinking.

But hey, at least you can pay six figures for your college education and emerge with crippling debt.

$$\oslash$$

Dennis Prager and Adam Carolla, whose "No Safe Spaces" appearances on college campuses are documented in the film of the same name, produced by Mark Joseph—are probably not the guys you would expect to be hitting the road together. What does a conservative Jewish intellectual (Dennis) have in common with a comedian who lived with a stripper, worked as a carpenter, and co-hosted *The Man Show* (Adam)? And why would *they* want to team up with the son of Christian missionaries who made a name for himself with his work on films *The Passion of The Christ* and *The Chronicles of Narnia* (Mark)?

Most people recognize Dennis Prager as a fixture on the Los Angeles radio airwaves since 1982; he has been nationally syndicated since 1999. His writings include *New York Times* bestselling books and a weekly syndicated column.

When Dennis was growing up in Brooklyn, New York, few would have pegged him as a future scholar.

In high school, Dennis was not just a class clown; he had his own chair named after him in the principal's office. He did the minimum amount of homework (none) and ranked in the bottom third of his class. On the other hand, Dennis wasn't the typical troublemaker, either. He took his schooling seriously enough to organize a student movement to crack down on cheating at his school. (The fact that this wasn't met with spitballs and wedgies from other students tells you all you need to know about how, even back then, people found Dennis pretty likeable.)

His parents, like his school, were Orthodox Jewish. But by Dennis's sophomore year of high school, they realized they would need to try an *unorthodox* parenting style with their son. They cut him a deal: Dennis would get a modest weekly allowance, and he could explore New York City and do as he liked—so long as he made it back to the family's Shabbat dinner table on Friday evening. It worked. Rather than waste his time and money, young Dennis explored classical music and Russian language and culture, studying both extensively on his own. During this time, he formed what would become a lifelong friendship with Joseph Telushkin, later a rabbi and leading Jewish thinker with whom Dennis would write *The Nine Questions People Ask About Judaism.*

When high school ended, Dennis's self-directed education had left him with less than stellar grades. With more selective schools out of reach, he enrolled at Brooklyn College. It ended up being a life-changing move.

There Dennis won the annual college award given to one of twenty-five hundred students in the sophomore class, a one-year scholarship to study anywhere in the world. He chose England. In April of that year he visited Israel, where friends arranged a meeting between him and representatives of the Israeli government. This meeting set his life on a new course.

At that time, the Cold War cast the shadow of possible nuclear war across the globe. The Soviet Union, still a formidable and dangerous Communist superpower, needed to maintain a veil of ignorance around its people. For Soviet Communists to stay in power, they had to hide the superior standard of living enjoyed in capitalist countries—and they needed to detain any would-be defectors who had seen life on the other side.

The Israeli government was looking for someone to smuggle Jewish religious items into the Soviet Union and to smuggle out names of Jews who wanted to defect to Israel. It was the perfect job for a devout Jew who had spent his free time studying Russian language and culture—in other words, it was the perfect job for Dennis, who also knew Hebrew. While it wasn't exactly the stuff of a Hollywood action movie, it was still a pretty risky endeavor. Dennis might not have been James Bond, but he was at least James Bondstein.

When Dennis returned to the United States after his adventures with Cold War intrigue, he started lecturing about his experiences. (In fact, the former class clown and middling student even became a college professor for a time.) After he moved to Los Angeles a few years later, his reputation as a speaker led to a Sunday night radio show about religion, which eventually grew into the daily, nationally syndicated *Dennis Prager Show*.

Dennis always recognized the need to keep growing his audience, reaching more and (more importantly) younger people. In 2012 he and his longtime producer Allen Estrin founded Prager University. In short, five-minute, online videos, Dennis and other lecturers would provide fact-based, easily digestible lectures on diverse topics such as politics, parenting, finance, and life skills.

PragerU doesn't have a brick-and-mortar location, and it can't give you an accredited degree. But if you are interested in learning and are intellectually curious, you can find information there that will expand your mind and extend your perspective. PragerU is a place for the pursuit of truth, knowledge, and clarity—a lifelong passion for Dennis.

By 2018, PragerU had a billion views a year, with 65 percent of its viewers under the age of thirty-five.

In 2011, when Dennis Prager interviewed podcaster and comedian Adam Carolla, he found someone who shared many of those passions and had arrived at many of the same truths, albeit via a wildly different path.

$$\oslash$$

Adam grew up in North Hollywood, California. After high school, he drifted into construction. He also taught boxing lessons on the side and took comedy classes at the Groundlings, the famous improv comedy troupe in Los Angeles. (Apart from a brief community college stint, those classes represented the closest Adam actually got to attending college.) He spent his free time doing stand-up comedy at open mic nights, sometimes standing in endless lines with dozens of other comics only to be turned away from the stage before he could perform.

In 1994, after hearing about a charity boxing match between Los Angeles area radio personalities, Adam showed up at the radio station and offered his training experience. He was tasked with mentoring a morning sports anchor named Jimmy Kimmel; they formed a connection that helped Adam break into comedy writing, and their friendship continues to this day. Adam reached a national audience when he was tapped to co-host the radio program *Loveline* with Dr. Drew Pinsky, which soon became a nightly staple on MTV. When giving relationship advice, he used his own observations from North Hollywood High, comparing the seemingly easy success enjoyed by students from strong, loving families with the lack of social mobility suffered by students (like himself) from broken homes.

After leaving *Loveline*, Adam joined Dennis on the airwaves as a syndicated radio host. His time on the air would not match Dennis's longevity, though. His show was cancelled in 2009 as part of a format change at his flagship station, KLSX Los Angeles.

Having built an audience over the years, Adam decided to try something that was quite new at the time. He launched his own podcast in February 2009, when the medium was still in its infancy, and no one had built a successful, stand-alone podcast. *The Adam Carolla Show* was an instant success, and the Guinness Book of World Records recognized it in 2011 as the most downloaded podcast. In the near-decade since its launch, Adam's single podcast has evolved into a profitable media network. And the best perk of all? No matter what he does or says, Adam can't get fired from this job.

$\oslash$

When Adam joined Dennis's show for an interview in 2011, it became immediately clear that despite taking very different paths in life, they shared important values.

Since they both value initiative, Dennis and Adam decided to do something about the free speech problem. So in 2012 they started appearing together on college campuses. If the faculty and administration wouldn't ask students to think critically, Dennis and Adam could bring the public forum to them.

Still, they couldn't bring that forum to each of the hundreds of colleges and universities across America...or could they? In 2016, they decided to film their experiences traveling from campus to campus. At that point, veteran producer and marketer Mark Joseph got involved. Mark, Dennis, and Adam chronicled Dennis and Adam's "No Safe Spaces" tour—a tongue-in-cheek reference to the insular bubbles that had been forming around college students for years—including their travel and their attempts to stimulate the American mind.

Mark, who is responsible for the "No Safe Spaces" title, had made a name for himself in multiple media forms—developing and marketing films such as *The Chronicles of Narnia*, producing *The Passion of the Christ: Original Songs Inspired by the Film*, serving as producer on films starring legends like Jerry Lewis and Martin Sheen, writing columns for HuffPost and *USA Today*, and authoring books on music, religion, and pop culture.

Originally Mark pitched actor and comedian Tim Allen (who had been a fan of one of Mark's previous movies), about the possibility of doing a docudrama together called *My Safe Space*. Ultimately Mark and Tim decided to pursue making a narrative movie about a president instead, which left this project still out there. Mark then connected with producer R. J. Moeller, who had originally connected Adam and Dennis (who had already been speaking on college campuses and were developing a film idea), and merged the two concepts.

The idea Mark wanted to convey with the title was simple: We already have a safe space, and it's called America. The First Amendment makes our country a safe space in which ideas can be shared freely. (Tim Allen agreed to join a comedy roundtable for the film.)

The official launch of the "No Safe Spaces" tour was December 1, 2016, at California State University, Northridge (CSUN), a public campus in southern California. We made the arrangements and began to get excited. What an opportunity this would be, to help students open their minds and their perspectives—to demonstrate that people from different backgrounds could find common ground and engage in an important dialogue. Even if people disagreed with what Dennis and Adam were saying, at least they would be talking, debating, and learning.

Then CSUN said Dennis and Adam were too controversial, and they cancelled the event. The gauntlet had been thrown down. That's when we knew we had to step up our game.

EXTRA CREDIT

In the course of making the *No Safe Spaces* film, Adam and Dennis had the chance to talk with some of the most insightful minds involved with academia today. Many of them are quoted in the book, but some of these conversations warrant extra attention. At the end of selected chapters, we'll include an "extra credit" section with some of the best ideas and concepts we encountered, told in the speaker's own words (with light editing for clarity) during the interviews.

CHAPTER TWO

SAFE SPACES VERSUS FREE SPEECH

alifornia State University, Northridge, didn't have a problem with either Dennis or Adam.

They didn't mind Dennis's background as a provocative conservative commentator. They didn't care that Adam had created and co-hosted a Comedy Central show that ended each weekly episode with scantily clad girls bouncing on trampolines. (And remember the "Juggy Dance Squad"?) CSUN knew all that was going on, and they *still* approved the two of them to show up. Adam and Dennis had already been to the campus a few years before, so the CSUN administration knew they didn't work (too) blue, didn't litter, and generally cleaned up nice.

For years, Adam had traveled to college campuses with Dr. Drew Pinsky, his former co-host on the popular radio show *Loveline*. School administrators had zero problem giving them a forum to answer questions about sex (threesomes, masturbation, venereal disease—you name it).

But when CSU discovered that they were talking about the need for more open-mindedness on college campuses?

That was a bridge too far.

Adam has something of a personal connection to California State University, Northridge. His mother graduated from CSUN with a degree in Chicano Studies (this despite the fact that she's whiter than Tom Petty).

In hindsight, given Adam's paltry parental upbringing, perhaps he and Dennis should have viewed the family connection to the school as a warning sign of impending doom. Maybe it shouldn't have surprised them when, after they were approved to be on campus and after six weeks of planning and preparation, CSUN pulled the plug—having figured out what the two of them wanted to talk about. CSUN claimed that they feared student protests and that "the scope and logistics around the event" were "just not feasible."

Scope and logistics?

When former presidents want to speak on a college campus (with their full security detail in tow), scope and logistics never seem to be a problem. Jimmy Carter is never turned away because of "scope and logistics" or because the university is afraid of a protest. In 2007 Former Iranian President Mahmoud Ahmadinejad took a break from threatening the end of America and denying the Holocaust ever happened to speak at Columbia University, right in the middle of New

York City. (Actually, he didn't take a break from those things—they were sort of part of his speech.) Somehow Columbia found a way to manage the scope and logistics.

Scope and logistics only seem to be a problem for certain types of speakers. The more closely you examine it, the clearer the pattern becomes.

Really, Dennis and Adam owe CSUN a great big thank you. The driving force behind the *No Safe Spaces* tour was a desire to talk about how close-minded academia had become. They never expected to have their point proven so quickly.

Adam and Dennis weren't the first speakers to be dis-invited by a college, and sadly they won't be the last. Administrators offer up innumerable excuses—"scope and logistics," "possible protests," "security," and so forth. They're just excuses, though. The reality is that some views are welcome on campus, and some aren't.

⊘

It sounds like an exaggeration, but colleges and universities really have gone downhill since the time when the *No Safe Spaces* speakers were ready to (in Dennis's case) matriculate or (in Adam's case) skip school to take up carpet cleaning. To appreciate how far off course higher education has drifted, imagine what an ideal classroom would look like.

Seems like an easy challenge, doesn't it? You go to college to imbibe knowledge and ideas. You learn how to be something: an architect or an engineer, maybe a doctor or a lawyer (if you put in some extra years). Your professors challenge you. They give you

information, and they ask you to think critically about it. They
encourage you to ask questions, and to constantly try to learn more.
Then you leave college and apply what you learned. Your college
experience gives you the know-how to do your job and puts you in
the right, inquisitive mindset to constantly get better. When you leave,
you're smarter than when you started.

According to Greg Lukianoff, President and CEO of the Foundation for Individual Rights in Education (FIRE)—an organization
founded to defend First Amendment rights on campuses—this concept of education is a relatively recent development.

There are few who understand the way free speech and campus
issues intersect better than Lukianoff. Before we go any further, it
is important to note that Lukianoff is no crazy right-winger. He
worked for the left-wing ACLU, did refugee work during the
Kosovo crisis, and used to work for an environmental mentoring
program for inner-city high school kids. And if that doesn't bolster
his liberal bona fides, he went to Burning Man for seven years. Yet
just like Adam (a pro-choice, pro-pot, atheist whose best friend is
Jimmy Kimmel) Lukianoff is now often taken for a right-winger.
All because he dares to work on behalf of free speech—something
once deemed a liberal value and celebrated by institutions like
Berkeley.

For most of history, higher education was dominated by religious
institutions providing religious training. "Some time in the nineteenth
century, particularly in the U.S., you start having these colleges
become these great centers of debate and discussion and innovation,"
Lukianoff explains. "The best parts of free speech. The best parts of
academic freedom. The best parts of scientific inquiry. And they

played an incredibly important role in an awful lot of progress in the last century."

According to Lukianoff, colleges have to provide that kind of open forum, or they aren't doing their jobs.

"It's supposed to be this bold environment for real inquiry that questions even sacred things in your society," said Lukianoff. "If you don't have that ethos, you can't really be effective at producing new ideas."

Lukianoff has been watching the struggle between freedom and comfort play out on college campuses since 2001, when he first joined FIRE as the group's first legal director.

Few organizations have been on the frontlines of academic freedom quite like FIRE has. The group was born out of *The Shadow University,* a 1988 book that exposed rampant political correctness on campus. The authors were Harvey Silverglate, a civil rights attorney who had previously led the Boston chapter of the ACLU, and Alan Kors, a professor at the University of Pennsylvania. After the book's publication, Silvergate and Kors figured that now they had exposed political correctness, the problem would take care of itself. Instead, they were inundated with requests from students looking for help in fighting illiberalism on campus. They founded FIRE to offer those people legal assistance.

For years, FIRE mainly focused on combating "speech codes"— guidelines that regulated who could say what and where and when they could say it. Realize (and this is important) that these guidelines were dreamt up and implemented by administrators—generally pencil-necked bureaucrats who were most interested in keeping order on campus and avoiding any bad publicity. After all, negative press could affect their next fundraising pitch to a corporate partner or a loaded alum. (Think Dean Wormer from Animal House, sitting in his office, putting John Belushi's fraternity on double super-secret probation just because he could.)

Cynicism aside, Lukianoff notes that these "speech codes" were at least hatched to help students. In the late 1960s and through the 1970s college campuses became more diverse. As student populations diversified—with more women, racial minorities, and other protected classes—cultures collided, and tensions arose.

"Some professors started believing that you should start passing progressive speech codes," explains Lukianoff. "So, there was this big movement to pass speech codes on campus that were aimed at racist and sexist speech on campus." But eventually, says Lukianoff, administrators went completely overboard. "Their definition of harassment," he says, "was essentially any unwelcome speech that you experience." Efforts to protect students from blatantly offensive speech quickly devolved into outright censorship when the definition of "blatant" and "offensive" got blurry. Overly cautious administrators found punishing "politically incorrect" speech the path of least resistance.

According to Lukianoff, until recently, FIRE had their hands full standing up for students and faculty in conflict with administrators over these ridiculous codes. "The best constituency on campus for free speech were the students themselves," says Lukianoff. "In particular, poorer students, minority students, and nontraditional age students. They seem to get it better than professors and definitely better than administrators."

That started to change in 2013 and 2014.

"The students themselves started demanding new speech codes, or that people not be invited to speak," says Lukianoff. Suddenly, students were demanding "trigger warnings"—a warning that something could be said that might "trigger" someone who suffers from post-traumatic stress disorder—for speech that might be controversial. They were demanding "safe space" where their precious ears wouldn't hear any offensive utterances, and they were demanding that certain topics be taboo.

A generation of administrators willing to silence speech had created a generation of students who saw no problem silencing speech. Imagine that.

But it gets even worse. Not content to let the administrators ostensibly running the campus enact speech codes, some radical student activists have no qualms taking matters into their own hands, violently if necessary. And, not surprisingly, the wishy-washy administrators who originally silenced speech to make sure everyone felt comfortable are hesitant to stand up to the loudest, angriest, most oppressive voices.

It's a strange turn of events.

The lefty University of California at Berkeley was once home to the Free Speech Movement. Hippie student activists who wanted to speak out about civil rights and the Vietnam War organized and pushed back against a ban on political activity on campus. (Yes, there was actually a time when colleges tried to keep politics from passing the campus gate. "Now, it sounds kind of naïve," muses Lukianoff.)

A little more than half a century later, Berkeley again found itself at the center of a free speech controversy. The question, once again, would be what can and cannot be said on campus.

Except that today students are the ones pushing for censorship. Maybe this generation of fascistic junior thought-police enforcers are rebelling against their hippie parents and grandparents' "anything goes" ethos.

In early 2017, the Berkeley College Republicans invited Milo Yiannopoulos to speak on campus. Yiannopoulos, at the time a writer for the conservative website Breitbart.com, was better known as a guy who lobs rhetorical bombs whenever he has a chance.

And some members of the Berkeley community figured the appearance would be a good time to throw real (smoke) bombs. Before Yiannopoulos even uttered a word, protests erupted across Sproul Plaza—the very section of campus where the Free Speech Movement had started fifty-three years earlier. Media reports estimated that over fifteen hundred protesters filled the plaza. At first they chanted and held signs—typical protest fare.

And then all hell broke loose.

Metal police barriers clanged to the ground, unable to hold back what was quickly becoming an angry mob. Protesters pelted police with rocks and fireworks. Black-clad activists, their faces covered like wannabe ninjas', heaved Molotov cocktails. The protest swelled into a riot, and then it spilled into downtown Berkeley, breaking windows and smashing storefonts.

Pranav Jandhyala, a member of the Berkeley College Republicans and a co-founder of BridgesUSA—a non-partisan campus group formed to bring a variety of guest speakers to Berkeley from across the political spectrum—was there.

"It was such a scary sight," Jandhyala recalls. As the protesters began dismantling police barricades, he began taking pictures and video. One of the masked, black-clad agitators saw him filming and tried to swipe his camera. Jandhyala managed to hang onto it, but he found himself crouched on the ground being pummeled with sticks and fists. He estimates the attack lasted for 15 or 30 seconds, and then, "I was able to scramble out of there." Jandhyala ran and kept running until he was off campus and clear of the danger.

Still foggy and confused, Jandhyala—a former high school football player—recognized that he had left the protest with a concussion. A friend drove him to the hospital for treatment.

The speech itself never even happened. Yiannopoulos was evacuated from campus for his own safety. Administrators, cowed by the demonstrations, threw roadblocks up in the way of subsequent conservative speakers. Ann Coulter and Ben Shapiro both had to reschedule events or change venues on campus because of security concerns.

"Scope and logistics" strikes again and again—as always, when the proposed speaker is a conservative.

⊘

FIRE's Greg Luikianoff gave the *No Safe Spaces* team a sobering analysis of the situation. It was sort of disheartening to hear, sitting in FIRE's downtown Philadelphia office, just blocks from where the Declaration of Independence and the Constitution were signed.

"Humans don't really like freedom of speech," Lukianoff told them, "they like to say they like it. And they definitely like their own freedom of speech. They don't necessarily like your freedom of speech that much."

And that attitude isn't limited to the campus thought police. People have been trying to talk over other people since two cavemen started smacking each other with clubs to see who would get to paint his stick figures on the side of a cave wall.

For that reason, Lukianoff says, the concept of free speech is actually quite fragile.

"The normal situation for most of human history is that the people or the person in charge gets to decide what is true," Lukianoff explains. "That gets enforced through things like beheading. You know, setting people on fire. Or burning them at the stake."

Things haven't gotten that bad on campus—at least not yet. (If that changes, we'll have a great excuse to make *No Safe Spaces II: Electric Boogaloo*.)

But the effort to turn modern colleges and universities into "safe spaces" at all costs sure does resemble the medieval despotism Lukianoff describes.

Lukianoff says that the lack of historical context has caused students to forget the role that free speech has played in advancing the values they claim to stand for.

"I feel like there's an entire generation of students who take freedom of speech, take the First Amendment so much for granted, they don't even understand that historically it has been the greatest protection of minority rights," says Lukianoff. (Maybe that says something about college history departments.)

The debate keeps returning to a very basic, very simple choice at the heart of higher education: Do we want colleges and universities to protect free expression and allow ideas to be aired, discussed, and debated? Or do we need to protect students from certain types of thoughts that they might find uncomfortable, hurtful, or otherwise offensive? It is a question we have to answer carefully because there are ramifications that don't stop at the campus gate.

As Dennis has repeatedly noted, liberty is a value, not a natural inclination. There's a romantic notion that all human beings yearn to be free. Not so. The greater yearning of the human heart is to be taken care of, not to be free. Freedom and liberty are ideas that must be taught and internalized. Sadly, America now has two or three generations (depending on how you count) who were raised to believe that being taken care of is more important than being free.

Part of feeling secure is staying away from difficult or challenging ideas. When we think about concepts outside our comfort zone—whether we're learning something new, trying to understand a complicated movie, or working through a disagreement with a loved one—it requires mental work. This work, this mental resistance, makes us stronger, so it's good in the long run. But in the short run, it takes effort.

It's easier to stay away from challenging thoughts. This is why conservatives watch Fox News and liberals tune in to MSNBC: it's more immediately satisfying to have your precious worldview validated. But the mind is like a muscle—without resistance, it gets weak. Watching and reading things that tell you how right you are all the time may feel great, but it turns you into a mental couch potato.

Academia, which exists to help correct our natural inclination to stick to ideas that feel safe, has instead allowed intellectual cowardice to fester.

"In fifty years of teaching—at Harvard, Stanford, NYU, Hebrew University, you name it—I have never met a group of less courageous people in my whole life than tenured Harvard and tenured other professors," said Alan Dershowitz.

Dershowitz may have gained fame as a defense attorney, but he minces no words while indicting his fellow law professors for their willingness to let students run amok.

"They are so terrified of their own shadow," he continued. "They don't want to do anything that upsets a student. They want their student evaluations to be very, very high."

Those student rankings have bitten Dershowitz.

"I was the most highly regarded classroom teacher for years at Harvard," Dershowitz told us. His scores dropped when he started sticking up for free speech. "I started making these points and then groups of students attacked my ratings. They would give me zero, zero, zero, zero in order to punish me for expressing my views."

If professors are on edge, you can imagine how jumpy administrators must be. The folks running each school have to worry about things like admissions and keeping those sweet, sweet donations rolling in from alumni and corporate partners. Bad PR isn't good for the gravy train, and student activists are exceptionally good at generating bad PR.

"Remember, too that a few handfuls of students can close down a university," Dershowitz observed. Those students don't even need to have much support among their peers. "The vast majority of students are not supportive directly of the radical Left. It's just that the radical Left has support from many faculty members [and] some administrators, and they can close down the university."

Picture a big school like the University of California at Berkeley or the University of Wisconsin. If ninety-nine students are minding their own business (hanging out in their dorm rooms, studying, sleeping, getting high, pondering reruns of *Spongebob Squarepants*), and only one social justice warrior decides to spend the day sitting cross-legged in the hall outside the provost's office singing "We Shall Not Be Moved," that one student's action can be enough to spur an official university response or a change in policy.

Lukianoff has seen this dynamic create a "weird and funny shift" in the types of cases people bring to FIRE. "Administrators have started coming to us in large numbers," he reports. "They want our help sort of putting the genie back in the bottle."

Ironically, Lukianoff explains, "In some cases, they authored these speech codes… [and] enforced them against their own students in fairly ridiculous ways. But now that they're actually seeing what happens when the students incorporate this idea of enlightened censorship, they're like, 'Help us make this stop!'"

That 1 percent taking over an administration building doesn't care what the other 99 percent have to say—unless they say the wrong thing.

EXTRA CREDIT: GREG LUKIANOFF ON THE IMPORTANCE OF FREE SPEECH

Plenty of people say they are passionate about free speech. But FIRE President Greg Lukianoff is someone who not only holds the right to free speech dear, but is steeped in knowledge and understanding of how freedom of speech has helped humanity evolve:

> I think free speech is one of the greatest innovations in
> human history. I think it's how we figured out how to have

peaceful, pluralistic societies that are endlessly creative and free. I think that free speech done correctly is one of the most exciting experiences you can have in your life. The idea that [you can] throw anything out there. We'll question anything. Let's figure stuff out. It's absolutely thrilling. And I also think that it's incredibly fragile.

If I thought that free speech would just be something that could defend itself I wouldn't be as worried about it.... You have to fight [for] that and you have to be aware that it's both precious and fragile. And I fear that we could lose it without even fully understanding that it's gone.

$$\oslash$$

One of the most basic things I feel like I have to explain about the First Amendment in particular is that you don't need a separate part of your constitution to protect the rights of a majority in a democracy. Everybody understood this at the time. Democracy—that protects the majority by the vote. The majority does not need a special amendment. The only reason why you have a First Amendment is to protect the rights of minorities, of people who aren't the majority. People who aren't in power.

That's why it's not a coincidence that the First Amendment was, believe it or not, not very strongly interpreted until about the 1950s. And it's not a coincidence. That's the time when you started seeing the real rise in the Civil

Rights Movement. In the Women's Rights Movement. In the Gay Rights movement. It's because people had tried to have these movements in the past, just with no [effective] First Amendment. With no freedom of speech, [those in power] would go, "Oh, you can't really have your protest Dr. King. You can't really have your rights protest yet."

But when the court started saying this is strongly interpreted you saw an awful lot of progress really, really quickly. And I feel like there's an entire generation of students who take freedom of speech, take the First Amendment so much for granted, they don't even understand that historically it has been the greatest protection of minority rights. Of the rights of the oddball. The rights of the underdog.

$$\oslash$$

I don't necessarily think you even need someone to be behind the movement to censor free speech. You need people sort of reverting to the normal sort of state of nature where I'm in charge, and I get to decide what you all can say. And that started happening on campuses. I even, you know, heard this very directly from someone who was an older professor saying, "When I was younger the conservatives always wanted to censor us. So, we're turning the tables now." No, no, no, no! That's not the goal. The goal is not to ever be going back and forth on this seesaw.... The idea is to get off the seesaw entirely.

The censorship instinct is so natural. All you have to do is nothing, and it sort of takes over on its own.

⊘

One of the results of this sort of "enlightened censorship" on campus is that students are not confronted sufficiently with people with whom they disagree.... And this is on the Left and the Right. They know what they're supposed to believe politically on the following positions. But then you ask them to explain why or defend themselves against basic arguments. They don't know. They have no clue why they believe it. They hold it just like John Stuart Mill said you would. If you're never challenged, you just hold onto your beliefs the same way people hold onto prejudices or superstitions. You know you believe them, but you haven't the faintest idea why.

Meanwhile working at FIRE, since we are actually an organization that makes a point of hiring people all over the political spectrum who actually argue with each other, my understanding of why I believe certain things got so much richer and deeper from these arguments. And yeah, one thing that people don't wanna do today, and they really should, is also be willing sometimes to let an idea go—say, "Wow, I guess I was wrong about that. I hadn't thought deeply enough about that." But that doesn't happen unless you have smart people with whom you can disagree, who can disagree with you without getting, you know, punished or being ostracized—or, for that matter being afraid of getting thrown out of school.

CHAPTER THREE

WHITE PRIVILEGE AND THE CULTURE OF VICTIMHOOD

H aving grown up a "gaijin" (the Japanese word for foreigner) in Japan, Mark has a pretty unique perspective on race. Because ethnic Japanese account for 98.5 percent of the population there, Mark knows more about being an ethic minority than most Americans, regardless of race. Japanese culture tends to repress such uncomfortable topics, but Mark's experience led him to believe that talking about race is almost always healthy. To the extent that race is so prominent in modern America, Mark feels like this is a good thing for our society. When people aren't allowed to talk about race (especially the politically incorrect stuff), it doesn't solve any underlying problems, it just cloaks them behind a façade of niceness. You never know for sure why you didn't get that job or apartment.

The good news is that Dennis and Adam don't shy away from such provocative discussions. When they visit campuses on the *No Safe Spaces* tour, they talk about Adam's "White Privilege." (Dennis usually brings it up. It seems to tickle him.)

As we have already explained, Adam hails from North Hollywood, California. Because the town has "Hollywood" in the name, it instantly conjures up images of glitz, glamor, and celebrity. Not so. There may have been one occasion when somebody spotted Robert Urich in the parking lot of a grocery store there. But other than that, the magical world of showbiz and *La La Land* could not be further away.

During his childhood, Adam's mother used food stamps and welfare to make ends meet. His father eked out a living but had almost no time or money for anything else.

When Adam finished at North Hollywood High School—North Hollywood High was a school you finished, not necessarily a place you graduated from—he rode his light skin tone right into a job cleaning carpets. There was no scholarship, no college, and certainly no freshman orientation speech telling him the world was his for the taking and that he could be whatever he wanted to be because he was special and unique in this world (just like everyone else). Instead, each night after the last patron had stumbled out of the Sizzler or Hamburger Hamlet and the joint had closed for the day, Adam and his colleagues would arrive and work until three or four in the morning, expunging the grime and spills and dirt left over from a day's worth of patrons. Glamorous stuff.

He parlayed that gig into a stint as a laborer on construction sites. Not a carpenter or an apprentice—a laborer. He spent years cleaning up garbage, digging ditches, pulling ivy off walls, and doing other chores that could just as easily have been assigned to a donkey, if a donkey could have answered the classified ad. (Lucky for Adam, it's tough to answer a classified ad when you're dialing the phone with hooves.)

It felt like his white privilege was broken (and there were no returns or exchanges).

During this time, Adam considered his future and thought he might make a good firefighter. He didn't know much about firefighters, but television had taught him that they should be strong, willing to risk life and limb, and enjoy hanging out between fires eating chili and playing foosball. Well, Adam was strong, he was eager to jump into the fray, and at the time had no family—so he had no qualms about risking his personal safety.

Oh, and he loves chili.

Adam traveled to the North Hollywood fire station to fill out an application to be a firefighter. When he turned it in, they told him, "Don't hold your breath. We won't be getting to you for a while."

For nineteen-year-old Adam, who was living in a garage with no real job and no real income, that might as well have meant, "Thanks, but no thanks." He proceeded to move out of the garage, work hard, and start a career as a carpenter (a job where he was almost certain he couldn't be replaced by a donkey).

Six years later, his father showed up to his apartment with a letter that the Los Angeles Fire Department had sent to his old house. They were finally inviting him to take a written exam to start the process of becoming a firefighter.

Now Adam had long since moved on from his dream of becoming a firefighter. Nevertheless, having already waited six long years, he decided to take the test anyway.

That Saturday, standing in line outside of North Hollywood High School, he started chatting with the people around him. One of those people was a short, slightly built female. Her ethnicity wasn't clear, but she appeared to be of mixed race like many people in the Los Angeles area.

"When did you put in your application?" Adam asked, looking to make small talk and commiserate about the six-year delay caused by the wheels of bureaucracy.

"Tuesday," she replied.

Forget about six years. She didn't even have to wait six days.

Does white privilege exist? Probably. The point is that it didn't exist for Adam. Moreover, it doesn't exist for most white people, the way professors and diversity administrators would have you think it does.

When Adam makes this point, he often gets some version of this reaction: "You don't see your privilege. You can't see it, because you're white." By this logic, some invisible force—unbeknownst to Adam—was clearing the patch ahead of him and pushing him along, giving him special advantages so that he could bask in the success of picking up garbage at a construction site.

And these same people who so confidently judge Adam for his supposed "white privilege" will turn around and admonish any white person who dares to talk about the experience of a person of color. How dare they assume they know what it's like for a member of the non-white community!

This selective outrage sends a couple of clear messages. First, white privilege makes white people blind to the advantages they receive—so if you're white don't presume to talk about your own experience. Second, white privilege makes white people blind to the real nature of other people's suffering—so, if you're white don't presume to talk about other people's experiences, either. In other words, if you're white, just shut up.

Welcome to the not-so-fun world of identity politics, which governs how colleges decide how students are allowed to talk about race—and which students are allowed to talk about it at all.

○

New York Times columnist Charles M. Blow is one of many leading black intellectuals who has discussed having "the talk" with his children. He tells them that people will be out to get them because of their skin color. He tells them the deck of life is stacked against them. And he tells them not to trust whites.

It's hard to imagine a more poisonous thing to tell a child.

Think about it this way. Adam has twins, a boy and a girl. If he were a less caring and loving father, that could make for some interesting experimentation. He could be published and lauded in psychological journals across the land—which he would have to read from a holding cell, once Child Protective Services got involved. Consider this hypothetical experiment: Each night, Adam ducks into his children's rooms to tuck them in and say good night. Each night, he tells one twin, "You're doing great. Tomorrow's going to be a wonderful day. The world is your oyster. You can be anything you want to be."

Then he tells the other twin, "People don't like you. It's going to be difficult for you to succeed. Don't set your sights too high. Becoming a doctor or lawyer is probably out of the question."

If Adam had these same conversations with his kids every night for years and years, how is the second twin going to turn out? She will be angry at society, distrustful of everyone, and closed off to anyone trying to offer help. That child will assume that everyone around her has sinister motives.

Unfortunately, this mindset—the victim mentality—is the foundation for how we discuss race in our society, especially on college campuses.

The victim mentality works this way: All people of color are victims of a system of oppression enacted by whites. White people are either actively oppressing minorities or passively oppressing them by existing within and benefiting from a system of "white privilege." So success or failure isn't the responsibility of the minority individual; black Americans win or lose with the hand that has been dealt to them from a deck stacked by white society.

It is easy to fall into the trap of victimhood. It certainly isn't limited to the dynamics between blacks and whites. This victim mentality pervades every strand of identity politics—radical feminism, gay rights, and rich versus poor, to name a few. Have you ever watched a sporting event with someone rooting for a different team? Say you're watching a Raiders-Chargers game; you're a Chargers fan, and your friend is pulling for the Raiders. By the time the second quarter rolls around, one of you will be complaining about the refs being part of a massive organized crime gambling syndicate. And the one who pipes up will be the one whose team is behind.

That's all well and good at the sports bar. But when that same mentality dominates important discussions about the real world, it becomes a problem.

Dennis's father, who served in the U.S. Navy during World War II, loved America. He constantly reminded Dennis and his brother how lucky they were to be growing up in America and how many opportunities they had. Yet, Max Prager had grown up in a world when Jews were banned from country clubs and blocked from joining law firms. (Imagine that: a world that banned Jews from becoming lawyers. The jokes must have been horrible.) Max's senior thesis at the City College of New York was on anti-Semitism in America. He knew exactly how tough Jews had it. But he also knew that his sons would live in a brighter future, instead of his difficult past. In fact, he told Dennis and his brother Kenneth (who became a professor of medicine at Columbia University) that they were the *luckiest* Jews because they were Jews who lived in America. Dennis has felt that throughout his life.

That message to his children was the polar opposite of the story of victimhood that young minorities and members of other "protected classes" receive today from parents and authority figures.

Dennis's grandfather was different from his father. The Prager grandfather had come to America from Austria in the late 1800s. He was convinced that just about every non-Jew was an anti-Semite. That might have been pretty close to true in Austria at the time, but sadly he brought that baggage with him to America. Any slight he suffered was chalked up to anti-Semitism. If someone cut him off in traffic, he'd complain about "the anti-Semite" driving in front of him.

That was funny to young Dennis, who wondered how the other driver could even know his Papa was Jewish. Tragically, what six-year-old Dennis laughed at has become the dominant mentality for many historically oppressed groups in America.

Thankfully, Dennis's dad made Dennis and his brother feel like the luckiest Jews in history—even while understanding that America had yet to fully live up to the American ideal.

⊘

Dennis's father was a lot like Shelby Steele.

A senior fellow at Stanford University's Hoover Institution, Steele doesn't mince words on the subject of slavery in America. Like Dennis's dad, he doesn't wear rose-colored glasses when he looks at America's past. He told us that slavery in America was particularly "inhuman" because of the overlap with the Industrial Revolution.

"In America you were brutalized," he said. "From birth onward you were whipped, lashed. Your children were taken from you and sold away. Your wives were used at the will of the overseer."

"It was just dehumanizing in every conceivable way—and for centuries."

The idea of people owning people was bad enough, and somehow America made it even worse than it sounds. Anyone who can read a history book has to acknowledge that slavery was bad; Steele has considered just how ridiculously bad it was.

But like Max Prager, he understands the difference between the future and the past.

"So, you got a beef. How long are you going to ride that beef?" he asked us, rhetorically. (Neither of us has a beef; but again, it was rhetorical.) "The only person who can break that bond is inside yourself."

As Steele told us, "Once you give up the idea of being a victim, all kinds of possibilities spring into play."

A victim mentality isn't only a crutch and an excuse for people whose ancestors were oppressed in the past, though. The white-guilt liberals and leftist ideologues who lead our colleges and universities seem more than happy to use the culture of victimhood to feed their own self-esteem. This phenomenon dates back to the 1960s—and the national political ideas that took root then and have grown into today's campus trends.

Steele saw it firsthand, having worked in three programs included in President Lyndon Johnson's "War on Poverty"—a quixotic effort to eradicate all forms of social inequality. The idea was to level the playing field for poor, lower-class people, including blacks and other minorities. In reality, these programs had terrible consequences for their supposed beneficiaries—but they continue to benefit the white liberals who implemented them. The point was to absolve them—and the Democratic Party—of their responsibility for sins of slavery and Jim Crow (the oppression of black Americans in the century after the Civil War).

"These programs are all designed to establish liberals, the Left in America, as the innocent party," Steele explained to us. "The liberals' welfare state tucked the sins of America's past—slavery, racism, lynching, Jim Crow laws, and the like—into the other side's baggage."

You saw this play out in the 2016 election. Democratic nominee Hillary Clinton boasted a record as a former Secretary of State and a former Senator. She had also been one of the most political, active, and significant first ladies in American history. But she didn't run on any of that. Instead she spent the majority of her campaign talking about the other candidate. Republican nominee Donald Trump was cast as a bigot, and she famously put half of his supporters (she didn't specify which ones) into a so-called "basket of deplorables."

The implications are clear, according to Steele: "If you vote for anyone on the other side, you are identifying yourself with one of the worst evils in human history."

The battle lines are drawn so boldly that race creeps into issues that have nothing to do with race, such as voter identification laws. People go bonkers over the notion that an identification card is required to vote. They call voter ID laws "voter suppression" tactics— as if they were the same as the literacy tests and violence that white racists wielded against blacks who tried to vote in the Deep South circa 1940.

First of all, if requiring you to show your ID is a method of oppression, then there is an awful lot of oppression going on in this country. Airports are full of oppression. Liquor stores? Oppression. Want to buy a pack of cigarettes? Hope you like your oppression extra smooth. Want to buy a car? Careful, oppression loses half its value the minute you drive it off the lot. Did you order something online at Wal-Mart and then go pick it up at the store? Well, congratulations! You got free two-day shipping and oppression. (One-day oppression costs an additional $9.95 per parcel.)

If access to a photo ID is an impediment to voting, then it's an impediment to an awful lot of other things in life. And how insulting is it to insinuate that minorities aren't smart enough to figure out how to get a photo ID?

And second, maybe it would be good to tap the brakes on comparing voter ID with the type of oppression that happened in the Jim Crow South (or in the North, for that matter, lest we only pick on the racists in one area of the country). When pickup trucks full of white-hooded Klansman were pulling up to polling places in 1932, they weren't there to check IDs.

But the worst part of the victimhood culture may not be in the non-issues it turns into issues but in the real issues it glosses over.

When commentator and author Van Jones appeared on Adam's podcast in 2017, he noted that victimhood mentality isn't limited to only one political ideology. And Jones definitely knows political ideology—he served as a key advisor to President Barack Obama and in 2005 founded The Color of Change, a grassroots organization dedicated to strengthening black voices in politics.

Yet Jones understands that pointing fingers doesn't solve anything.

"Both sides of the aisle are in a race for victim status, Left and Right," Jones told Adam. "They seem to be forming identities based on victimhood, and they get points based on their ability to articulate their victim status. They don't get points based on solving problems."

Victimhood mentality blames "white privilege" for the plight of American minorities. Privilege does indeed exist in America today, but it is not white privilege. It's "two-parent" privilege.

Study after study has shown the long-term socioeconomic benefits children enjoy when they come from a stable two-parent household. Kids who grow up in a home without a father are four times as likely to end up poor as are kids in two-parent homes. Kids who grow up in a two-parent household have a lower risk of teen pregnancy. They do better in school, and they commit less crime. And according to the Brookings Institution people who finish high school, hold down a full-time job, and wait until they are at least twenty-one to get married and have kids (in that order) avoid poverty at a 98 percent clip—regardless of race.

Statistics prove this, but so does the petri dish of North Hollywood High School. Adam spent his high school years watching different cliques. The kids from strong families with two-parent homes, who had someone telling them to do homework and stay out of trouble, went on to college and were set up for successful careers. Adam and his friends, who mainly came from single-parent homes just getting by, wound up cleaning carpets and competing with donkeys for jobs on construction sites.

In the black community, two-parent households are becoming an endangered species. Census data reveal that about 40 percent of all American children (regardless of race) are born out of wedlock; that number jumps to 53 percent for Hispanics and 71 percent for blacks. The Great Society programs of the 1960s, which did nothing to cut the poverty rate, implemented rules that inadvertently punished two-parent households, creating a disincentive for families to stay together.

As a result, black children today are less likely to grow up with their mother and father than black children born during the time of slavery.

Shelby Steele pointed out that the problem is guilt-fueled, shortsighted policies, from politicians with no qualms about milking the victimhood culture to win elections. "They throw all these goodies at black people," he said, "without taking into account the damage it does to [them]."

Even worse than the smarmy politicians are the faculty and administrators on campus who sit neck-deep in the warm, soothing mud bath of what used to be called white liberal guilt, resting their identity and outsize self-esteem firmly on the proposition that they are the white knights rushing to the rescue of the approved victims. They completely dismiss anyone who points out societal factors holding racial minorities back from success. Surrounded by well-funded diversity departments (see Chicano Studies at CSUN), they'll happily tell anyone who will listen about the horrors of white privilege.

If you dare to identify cultural impediments to minority success— no matter how sound your statistics or how thorough your research— you are branded a racist. Suddenly you wake up as the literary love child of Kafka and Hawthorne, wearing a scarlet "R" around your neck.

That's if you have the misfortune of being white. If you're black and you bring up these issues, surely that would help your case, right?

"They say, 'You're not black,'" Steele told us. "'You're an Uncle Tom. You're a sellout.'"

By silencing critical voices, they ensure that they don't have to engage with any uncomfortable, challenging ideas.

But by avoiding ideas and evidence that seem dangerous to them, they're courting some real dangers for the very people whose cause they purport to champion—and to our society at large. As they keep beating the same drum, telling millions of Americans that their race puts a target on their back, do they ever consider the consequences?

If you believe that you're oppressed and everyone is out to get you, why try harder to get a better job? If it's been drilled into your head that the police want to hurt you, why not fight back if a cop pulls you over?

But critics of the victimhood mentality aren't just on a different side—they're cast as evil. Ku Klux Klansmen. Nazis. And in civil discourse, you don't bother engaging those types of extremists. If you're discussing race relations and an actual Klansman sidles up to the table and says, "Hey, I've got a few two-by-fours and a can of gasoline that could help solve this problem," you don't ask him to explain his position. You tell him that intimidation and violence are not the solution to any problem, and you tell him to leave. You don't even validate his parking.

But opposition to the idea that racial minorities are oppressed in this country is not KKK ideology. If you paint that kind of reasonable disagreement with the same brush as violent extremism, at best you're squashing debate. At worst you're prompting a violent backlash.

We find that the best answer is to show up and talk about common sense. People aren't used to polite opposition. On the *No Safe Spaces* tour, we've had our run-ins with those ready to label us as racist.

Adam likes to remind people that if he were a racist, he wouldn't make so many racist jokes. After all, if he were secretly gay, deep in the closet and leading a double life, would he talk to his wife about interior design and dress patterns? Or would he grunt, scratch himself, and go move some two-by-fours around the yard? (By the way, has there ever been a better time than today to be an actual honest-to-goodness racist? Think about it. If you were a racist fifty years ago, you were running with the people who were burning crosses, bombing churches, or spraying civil rights demonstrators with fire hoses. Not the best company, putting it mildly. Today, actual racists get lumped in with Adam, Dennis, and some other very esteemed mainstream people. That's much better company, right?)

Whenever Dennis schedules a campus appearance, some columnist for the campus newspaper calls Dennis a bigot, a racist, a homophobe, a sexist, an Islamophobe—if it ends in -ist or -phobe, they use it. At the University of Wyoming, they even called him an anti-Semite, which shows you the crack research that goes into concocting the word soup they spew out.

Despite giving longer responses than questioners might expect, Dennis has a straightforward style of speaking. He speaks truths. While many people will pull their punches, afraid of offending people, Dennis is like a doctor who diagnoses a patient without concern for race, gender, ethnicity, or sexual orientation. He just offers his opinions and assumes other adults can handle them—and argue back if they disagree. He presents the truth, without varnishing it for one group or another. That's the opposite of bigotry. Dennis is actually one of the least hateful people you'll ever meet.

So when a student at the University of California-Santa Barbara wrote his own version of the "Dennis the Racist Menace is Coming to Campus" article, Dennis invited the columnist on his radio show. It turned out that all this kid knew about Dennis was that he was a conservative; he had assigned a negative connotation to that label because of all the scare stories about evil, racist conservatives that he had heard in his classes and on his campus. As a result of appearing on Dennis's show where Dennis treated him with his characteristic civility, the columnist attended Dennis's talk, and later wrote a follow-up piece in which he apologized and said he had been wrong.

See? It's so much nicer when we make an effort to talk out these misconceptions.

We are not suggesting that racism doesn't exist in America today. Of course, it does, and it is every bit as wrong and ugly as it ever has been.

But it's also rare. Professors have to resort to theories of involuntary racism—"white privilege," "systemic racism," "institutional racism," and so forth—because the overt and obvious racism of the past is now unacceptable. What do you think would happen to a restaurant that refused to serve Hispanic and Latino customers today?

The truth is, times have changed—and for the better. Back in 2013, Mark wrote a column for *USA Today* titled: "No, Oprah, America Isn't Racist." The piece was in response to an interview Winfrey had given to the BBC, in which she attributed a lot of the opposition to then-President Barack Obama to racism. Mark was making the point that even though racism had obviously not been eradicated, much progress had been made and a lot of colorblind Americans (people who came of age in a post–Dr. Martin Luther King era) had not only made Winfrey into a huge TV star, they had elected Barack Obama in the first place. "Oprah is still living in that other time and era in which people separated themselves from one another primarily on the basis of race—a real time to be sure," Mark conceded, "but one that is, for the most part, not our reality today. That's especially so at the highest levels of politics and entertainment."

Shelby Steele advocates getting to a place where the response to the idea of racism is, "So what?" His "so what" mentality may sound at first like it devalues the struggle for equality, but in reality it's a very empowering concept.

Taking personal responsibility is always the best way to handle this type of adversity. No playing field is ever fully level, but if you're the one running, you still decide where to go. If you go to a restaurant at 6 o'clock on a Friday night and it's closed, you can blame the restaurant ("Who closes at six on a Friday night?"), or you can tell yourself that next time you'll check to make sure it's open before you jump in the car and drive somewhere.

In one case, you're hoping someone else will do the right thing. In the other case, you're directing your own life, even if someone else does something stupid. Guess which path is going to be more successful?

EXTRA CREDIT: DAVE RUBIN ON FREE THOUGHT AND INDIVIDUALISM

As a married gay man, Dave Rubin, host of *The Rubin Report*, is living a life that should have progressives cheering for him. So why aren't they? He had a lot to say when he sat down and discussed identity politics and individualism with Dennis:

> We've gotten to a point where if you say you're tolerant all the time, if you talk about diversity all the time and tolerance all the time, people somehow think that means you are tolerant, and you care about diversity. And in almost every case, almost without fail, today, that's actually the reverse.
>
> So right now, it's very "in" for everyone on the Left to talk about tolerance and diversity and all these things. And what is the type of diversity that they hate? Well, the type of diversity that they hate is diversity of thought. So we like

black people as long as black people think the way we think they should think. We like Muslim people as long as they think the way we think they should think.

This is actually the essence of prejudice, really, because prejudice means to prejudge. So if you look at someone, and you think that you know how they should think by their immutable characteristics, I mean, this is the reverse of everything that Martin Luther King Jr. wanted.

This monster, this corrosive way of thinking—and as I said, really lazy way of thinking—has affected the gay community tremendously, because the gay community was fighting for equality for a long time. I mean, you know me. I want equality. I want equality under the law. I don't want any special treatment. I don't want any special favors or to be looked at differently. If you give me equality… then we can all treat each other as crappily as we treat everybody else.

Now, what's happened is the gay community fought for equality for so long that in an odd way, they've become addicted to the pain of that. So it's an extension now. You can't just let it go. To me, it's like, look, we got equality and now I can sit down across from you and all these scary conservatives and right-wing maniacs that everyone will say you guys are, and you're not fighting to take away my equality. We got a win, and we have to be appreciative of a win.

$\oslash$

If you understand that you own your mind, that your life is yours, you have to go out and get things. No one gave me anything. I don't think anyone gave you anything. Yes, some of us are born into a little bit more, but plenty of people that are born into a lot lose a lot. And some of us have come with nothing and make it, and then lose it and make it again....

The idea of pain and being addicted to it goes right to the heart of all of this. This is about individualism and fighting for your own capacity to think and create a society that you want to live in, not one that's just thrust upon you.

○

Liberalism really is about the individual, and it's about live and let live. We believe in this kind of liberalism. It's not just this amorphous idea of tolerance. That's a collectivist view of the world where we should be grouping all of these people, and we should be taking from some and giving to others. And it is a snake that will eat its own tail. It cannot sustain itself.

And we see all the time, the reason that people are coming to people like me right now, it's not because I'm saying anything that I think is that groundbreaking, actually. It's that I'm telling them some simple truths to allow them to escape brainwashing. Because leftism is brainwashing. That's all it is. It doesn't teach you how to think. It teaches you to think what they want you to think. And that's incredibly dangerous. So being liberal now, which in essence means live and let live, I know, you know, people think that's really a libertarian position, but that's truly what liberalism is....

This is the only way we can function. We live in a society of 350 million some-odd people. They're supposed to think different things. But the Left is trying to beat everyone into thinking the same thing.

$$\oslash$$

When I go to these schools, what I find most interesting is that when we open it up to the Q & A at the end, the kids that are coming up and asking questions [are] almost like refugees from a mental institution. They're asking the most basic questions about, "Can I speak?"

The question I get most is, "If my professor believes in all of this postmodern leftist nonsense, and I want to voice my opinion, my grades are going to be hurt." And when I started doing the college thing about two years ago, I used to say, just suck it up while you're in school and get the grade so you can hopefully get to grad school or get the job you want and then deal with it. And I've had a complete 180 on this....

If you compromise then, you don't just magically get out of college. Now you've got a wife and a kid and other pressures, and you've got to pay property taxes, and all kinds of other stuff. You don't suddenly magically get brave. It's pretty rare that you magically get brave.

CHAPTER FOUR

IN WHICH WE MANSPLAIN FEMINISM AND GENDER POLITICS

I n 2014, Wellesley College had a peculiar visitor.

Students at the all-women's college outside Boston saw a paunchy, middle-aged, balding man who appeared to be staggering across their campus in a zombie-like state. With eyes closed and arms outstretched like a cartoon version of Frankenstein's monster, he was wearing only a pair of tighty-whities.

"The Sleepwalker" was actually a piece of art. Well, it was a sculpture. Calling a flabby, pasty-skinned depiction of mid-life decline "art" is the height of irony. Built of epoxy and painted with lifelike skin tones and features, he garnered a few double takes. He probably attracted his share of chuckles, too.

But some students were deeply offended by "The Sleepwalker."

Two of them started a petition to remove the statue. Their reason? The realistic depiction of a nearly naked man could "trigger" survivors of sexual assault.

Wellesley College, to their credit, refused the petition and left the statue up until they removed the rest of the art installation.

This may seem like an odd reason for someone to complain about a statue. But the Wellesley students' reaction to the statue fits within the broader discussion of sex and gender on campus. Like other discussions that occur on college campuses, it leans heavily on emotional appeals—less so, on facts.

⊘

Take the widespread belief that college campuses are permeated by a "rape culture."

This term alludes to a dubious statistic that one out of five college women will be the victims of sexual assault.[1] Then Vice President Joe Biden even mentioned this statistic during a video shown at the 2016 Democratic National Convention, using the authority of his high office to spread it to a national audience. If the statistic were true, it would be alarming, to say the least.

However, this statistic is based on highly suspect data.

The 20 percent number comes from a voluntary survey conducted by the Department of Justice of five thousand respondents at two large universities. Respondents were asked a series of questions, and then the people administering the survey—not the respondents themselves—determined who was a victim of "sexual assault." And even the researchers conducting the survey—citing a low response rate—said that the results couldn't be used to diagnose an epidemic on college campus. None of the claims made in the survey were independently investigated or confirmed. The results don't indicate who voluntarily opted into the survey and who didn't, which creates a skew of its own.

And really, is 20 percent a realistic number? That's shockingly high. If one in five women were really assaulted on campus, wouldn't enrollment have cratered at some point? Who would send their daughter off to college if there was a 20 percent chance that she would be sexually assaulted?

There's good news and bad news. The bad news: the United States Bureau of Justice Statistics (which, for obvious reasons, gathers its data much more carefully) estimates that one in 52.6 women will be sexually assaulted during her time in college.[2] That's way too many, and campuses should be working to eradicate this threat.

The good news is that 1.9 percent is much lower than 20 percent.

Even the language surrounding sexual assault gets muddied. When you hear that someone was sexually assaulted, it sounds like a technical legal term for rape or attempted rape. Yet when people talk about sexual assault on campus, they can also be referring to behaviors such as "unwanted kissing."

Let's be perfectly clear here: non-consensual sexual behavior—including unwanted kissing (or what used to be called a guy getting fresh with his date)—is not ok. Those actions should have consequences. Maybe that requires involving authorities. A slap in the face, or a well-placed knee to the groin, could also be appropriate.

Yet there is a wide chasm between unwanted kissing and attempted rape—and that chasm is not reflected in the catch-all term "sexual assault." Driving 45 in a school zone is not the same thing as vehicular homicide. Sure, they're both moving violations. Sure, they're both dangerous. As a society, however, we recognize that these offenses are not the same level of severity and therefore handle them differently. That's why zero-tolerance policies for anything are asinine.

It's great that campus authorities want to make it clear that non-consensual behavior is unacceptable. It's not great that they're doing it in a way that puts uncomfortable annoyances on the same level as violent crimes. They don't want anyone shrugging off unwanted kissing or groping. Therefore they label it all sexual assault and drop it in the same bucket as rape. If you try to kiss a girl who doesn't want to be kissed, they're telling their male students, you're in the same Uber pool as someone who physically overpowers and violates another person.

Do you see how this can create problems?

To some degree, that strategy is successful—people take a wide range of unwanted sexual behaviors more seriously than in the past. But conversely, people are starting to taking rape *less* seriously. When someone reports a sexual assault, the range of what that could mean is so wide that people aren't sure what response is appropriate. If everyone is a predator, eventually no one is a predator.

It isn't enough for an action or a behavior to be bad. It has to be the worst thing ever.

You saw this in the final days of the 2016 election, when an eleven-year-old audio recording surfaced of Donald Trump bantering with *Access Hollywood* host Billy Bush. You remember this recording, so we're not going to go into graphic detail. Trump bragged about his sexual prowess and how women would let him do anything he wanted because of his celebrity status. It was disgusting, gross, and entirely unpresidential. (Disclosures: In 2008, Adam predicted [on air] that Trump would become president. Later, Trump "fired" Adam from *The Apprentice*. He's not bitter, though. Nope. Not even a little bit. Not in the least.)

Then, as disgusting as the audio recording was, Trump's enemies somehow managed to blow it out of proportion. They characterized it as bragging about sexual assault.

Bragging that your luck with women comes from your celebrity status? Sad! (To quote a certain president.) Trump was basically admitting, *If I was just a developer from Queens, women wouldn't give me a second look. I'd be a creepy sixty-year-old guy. But I'm on television, so I do all right.* How is that in any way impressive?

More important, he was talking about *consensual* sex. His celebrity status meant women would "let you do" ... well, you remember. And his claims were almost assuredly exaggerated. That's the way these conversations go. That's the way guys operate when we talk to other guys: we always try to make it sound like our luck with women is better than it really is.

Trump passed it off as immature locker room talk. There's a legitimate argument that a potential President of the United States should not be saying such things. A sixty-year-old guy should know better, anyway. That might say something about his judgement, or how he views other people. That's certainly worth talking about.

Instead, Trump's critics escalated the scandal to create an accusation of sexual assault. And that changed the conversation completely:

Instead of deploring what Trump actually said, we were arguing about what he did or didn't say. (Incidentally, changing the conversation that way let Trump off the hook.)

The fact is, handling allegations of sexual assault and harassment becomes increasingly difficult when behavior that obviously isn't either of those things is injected into the discussion.

And that's the strategy on college campuses. It turns out campus feminists love to twist language. They've created an entire lexicon of words and phrases that sound like Herbert Marcuse found a cheat code on *Words with Friends*.

⊘

Take "toxic masculinity."

Remember when we discussed white privilege? Well, just as white people are excluded from any discussion of race because of some subconscious, built-in societal advantage that drastically changes our outlook, men are also disqualified from speaking out. If you're a man, you can be judged guilty of spreading toxicity just by being you.

The theory behind the concept of toxic masculinity is that traditionally accepted male roles dispose men to aggression and violence, so that they create unsafe environments for women, gays, lesbians, and other marginalized groups. Men who try to act in too manly a way will shout down women and make them too uncomfortable to share their opinions. Ironically *invoking* toxic masculinity has that very effect. It shuts down open dialogue—just in reverse.

(Oh, you disagree? Well, shut up. I'm trying to tell you exactly how you silence others.)

Like many examples of political correctness, there's a kernel of truth in the idea of toxic masculinity. Guys can sometimes be jerks. That's a fair point. But the "toxic masculinity" goes off the rails blaming all obnoxious male behavior on traditionally male roles and activities. Aggression, ambition, and competitiveness—qualities hardwired into men through years of evolution so they could (a) attract a mate, and (b) find food and shelter for their families—are supposed to explain a wide range of social ills. Again, it's a case of putting very different things in one catch-all category. Did a lunatic shoot up a shopping mall? Blame the toxic masculinity that taught him to be overly aggressive. Did a construction worker whistle at you? That, too, was toxic masculinity. He saw you as a sexual conquest.

What if you're a man, and you want to push back and assert that your masculinity is non-toxic? Well, then you're "mansplaining." That's a fancy word for a male asserting himself in a discussion with a woman.

There are some parallels with the discussion of racial identity politics. Feminists will claim they are empowering women by blurring the language and casting men as perpetual aggressors. The other side of this coin, though, is that women are cast as perpetual victims. "Mansplaining" can only be a threat if women are perceived as too weak to hold their own in a conversation.

The same is true of "the patriarchy," the hairy, sweaty, vast conspiracy of men who really run the world and preserve male dominance. These fellows' subliminal control over everyone's mind is the sole reason why Geraldine Ferraro isn't on the $10 bill today.

It's also the reason so many women get trapped in antiquated domestic relationships, where they are forced to do repressive things like have kids and start a family.

$$\oslash$$

Speaking of repressive norms, let's talk about family.

Let's say you could choose one of two guaranteed outcomes for your life. For the purposes of this exercise, choosing one does not mean the other will not happen, but only one can be guaranteed.

Would you choose the promise of a great marriage or the promise of a great career?

Dennis likes to ask this of students, and he asked Olivia Corn (a junior at Cornell University) this very question during the *No Safe Spaces* tour. At the time, Corn had recently finished a term as president of the school's College Republican club. Like many politically conservative women, she chose the guarantee of a great marriage.

There is a notable split in answers to this question based on the responder's ideology. More left-leaning women will pick the career—focusing on independence and seeing professional success as the means to get there.

Apparently they're influenced by the folks at the front of the classroom. Corn told Dennis that if she gave the same answer in class, her professors would challenge her.

"They probably would have asked why," said Corn. "They would have questioned it a bit and asked why career wasn't my primary focus." Feminists consider the traditional family structure (husband, wife, kids, and maybe a pet) to be a system of repression. That white picket fence on *Leave it to Beaver* might as well have had barbed wire and an electric current to keep Mrs. Cleaver slaving away in the kitchen.

Campus feminists talk a big game about choice, and about respecting all women. But they lack patience for women whose choices include building a family, or who don't share their left-leaning political views.

"If you're a conservative woman," mused Kassy Dillon, "you no longer have a uterus, according to all these leftists."

She said that to Dennis during her senior year at Mount Holyoke College, back in December 2017. Now she writes for the Daily Wire, a conservative website. Before that, she founded Lone Conservative, a website for right-leaning college students who felt philosophically isolated on campus.

Dillon knows just what it's like to be philosophically isolated, especially in an environment that should be welcoming by design.

Mount Holyoke is one of two women's colleges located in the scenic Pioneer Valley in Western Massachusetts. (The other is Smith College; they are two of five colleges located within a fifteen-mile radius of each other.) Theoretically, this should be a place where true feminism should be strongest, where women can be free to intellectually explore and develop their thoughts and philosophies about life, right?

Not so, Dillon told Dennis. She described how her conservative views meant more scrutiny of her classwork.

"I need to put in twice as much work," she explained, telling Dennis about writing papers for hostile professors. "I need to cite more sources. I need to make a stronger argument. I need to go over that page limit."

It doesn't stop in the classroom, either.

"I've had my friends, who have been seen on campus with me, get confronted by other people," said Dillon. "Even my roommate, she got harassed."

"You can't be friends with 'the Republican girl.'"

$\bigcirc$

Gender politics gets even more fun when colleges bend over backwards to accommodate "transgender" individuals.

Even places like Mount Holyoke, with an all-female student population, aren't immune to complications. During Dillon's freshman year, Mount Holyoke's administration decided (without consulting the campus community) to admit biologically male students who identify as female. Barnard College in New York City has a similar policy. "Identifying" as female carries no requirement for any kind of medical diagnosis, so long as the candidate consistently calls himself (sorry, herself!) female.

What happens if a female student comes to Mount Holyoke and then decides to identify as a male? That student is allowed to stay at the all-female campus, with the justification that it is safer.

If you're scoring at home, a quick recap: if you're born a male and then decide to identify as female, you're allowed to attend the all-female college because of your self-identification, regardless of your biology. If you are born a female, show up at Mount Holyoke, then decide to identify as male, you're allowed to attend the all-female college because of your biological sex, regardless of how you identify.

You can count Dillon as one of the students who isn't buying it.

"If you are allowed to go to an all-women's college while identifying as male, is your claim to being a male actually valid?" she asked Dennis, rhetorically. It's a reasonable question that deserves an answer. A student who decides to attend a single-sex college has a certain expectation about the makeup of the student body. When the makeup of the student body changes, the people paying tens of thousands of dollars should at least get an explanation.

Yet for asking such questions, Dillon was at higher risk of getting kicked out of Mount Holyoke than the hypothetical gender-switching student who identifies as male at a women's college. (Come to think of it, it's probably a good thing for Dillon that we're publishing this well after her graduation.)

⊘

The perverse results of gender politics on campus have been enabled by Title IX of the Education Amendments of 1972.[3] Title IX is a federal law that, on its face, simply prohibits discrimination based on sex from any educational activity at an institution of higher learning that receives federal funds.

Over the nearly five decades since its surely good-intentioned inception, Title IX has had many unintended consequences. For example, the law was interpreted to require schools to spend an equal amount on men's and women's sports, even if men's sports drew more participation (and money). Since sports that aren't men's basketball—and, for big schools, football—tend to be money pits, colleges and universities achieved that balance by nixing programs like wrestling and men's gymnastics.

Meanwhile, mission creep has put campus authorities in the position of adjudicating claims of sexual assault and harassment. Supreme Court cases in the 1990s (*Franklin v. Gwinnet County Public Schools* and *Davis v. Monroe County Board of Education*) and Department of Education policy—particularly under the Obama administration— have encouraged school administrators to view this quasi-legal realm as part of their responsibility. When allegations arise, regardless of what happens with off-campus authorities, on-campus judicial boards mete out their own punishments.

When handling allegations of a crime, off-campus authorities have to pursue evidence, respect procedure, and protect the rights of both the accuser and the accused. On-campus judicial boards have no such responsibilities, and they too often become politically correct kangaroo courts more interested in protecting the school's reputation than in getting to the truth about an allegation.

You can see this in two high-profile cases. In 2014, the University of Virginia temporarily suspended all fraternities and sororities when *Rolling Stone* published the gripping, horrific, and (as was discovered later) false tale of a student who had been gang raped at a Phi Kappa Psi party. In 2006, Duke University forfeited its lacrosse season, suspended several members of the Duke men's lacrosse team, and forced the coach to resign after allegations (again, later proven false) that teammates had raped a stripper during a party.

But the cases don't always make sensational national headlines. In 2013, an Amherst College disciplinary board expelled a male student after his girlfriend's roommate accused him of rape. "John Doe" (the anonymous male student) maintained his innocence, but despite her shifting story, the board decided that the accuser's version was probably true. That's not an exaggeration, either: the burden of proof required for a disciplinary board to take action in this case was "a preponderance of evidence," which in layman's terms mean that the evidence says the accusation is more likely than not. Had this happened in a court of law, a prosecutor would have to prove John Doe's guilt "beyond reasonable doubt." There's a big difference. But at Amherst college, 51 percent was good enough.

And 51 percent meant that John Doe got booted off campus, lugging around his neck a transcript that told the world he had been expelled for disciplinary reasons. Even when he managed to find new evidence—text messages from the accuser that suggested their coupling was, in fact, consensual—the school refused to back down.

The preponderance of evidence standard came right from the Department of Education. In a 2011 letter to college administrators known as the "Dear Colleague Letter," the Assistant Secretary of Education in charge of (ironically) Civil Rights encouraged colleges to aggressively pursue punishments for sexual assault and harassment, regardless of whether the alleged behavior even takes place on campus or during a school-sponsored activity or program. This conceivably puts private interactions between adults in an off-campus apartment within the jurisdiction of these campus boards. In fact, the Dear Colleague Letter encourages schools to take action "[r]egardless of whether a harassed student, his or her parent, or a third party files a complaint under the school's grievance procedures or otherwise requests action on the student's behalf." You don't even need to be accused to be tried.

The Dear Colleague Letter also explains that "because the standards for criminal investigations are different, police investigations or reports are not determinative of whether sexual harassment or violence violates Title IX." Those centuries of legal tradition built up around the concept of due process? No need to worry about that.

Oh, and by the way, the letter says that schools don't have to let you have a lawyer present, either.

And in case you forgot, this document—which suspends your due process, limits your access to an attorney, and allows extra-judicial entities to punish you with no oversight or appeals process—comes from the Department of Education's Office of Civil Rights.

$\oslash$

College could be a valuable experience for young men and women who are transitioning from adolescence into the real world of adulthood.

When young people turn eighteen, they enjoy more freedom in the eyes of the law and in the eyes of society. Part of growing up is handling that newfound independence and being responsible enough to make the right choices that might curtail your freedom.

For example, up through high school, your parents may wake you up each morning to ensure you go to school. They're in charge of making sure you eat right and yelling at you when your behavior is unacceptable.

When you leave the nest, these things become your responsibility. You have to learn how to get to class on time. You have to figure out how to buy and prepare your own food. You have to learn how to interact with other people without acting like a jerk.

In fact, learning how to interact with other people, especially with people of the opposite sex, is one of the most important lessons that people learn during this time of their lives.

What messages are students hearing during these formative years? Women hear that men are out to get them (either consciously or subconsciously). Men (the two of us, at least) observe firsthand that most women don't want to talk to us, and that even the most seemingly benign overtures can now be construed as harassment. Campus feminists teach that women who marry and start a family deserve pity, that they have been duped, and that they have surrendered any hope of happiness.

That's more than a bleak outlook—it's downright poisonous.

You can see the effects in modern romantic relationships. Many younger adults have turned to phone apps for dating, rather than approaching people in public and risking an awkward situation. You've heard the phrase "wouldn't lift a finger" to describe the bare minimum that someone can do? Well dating apps have lowered the bar. You can now date and literally not lift a finger—just swipe.

A new dialect of English exists to describe the peculiarities of this risk-free, conflict-averse modern dating environment. Worried that your crush won't reciprocate your feelings? You might try "benching" a few prospective boyfriends, stringing them along just in case. Don't want to create a tearful scene during a breakup? Try "ghosting" your significant other—simply never contact her again and ignore any calls or texts. The fall is the start of "cuffing season," when people jump into superficial relationships so that they have someone to bring home for Thanksgiving or watch Hallmark Christmas movies with.

These weakly bonded, ad-hoc relationships have led to more casual sexual relationships and contributed to the trend of people getting married later in life. The result is an extended adolescent period. It's not just that people are coming out of college with a poor understanding of how to enter into and nurture a relationship; it delays their adulthood and makes them less-productive members of society.

If you want to know exactly how confused young people are, here's the cherry on top: in 2016, Florida Atlantic University released a study that found that people in the twenty- to twenty-four-year-old age range are having less sex. The tools and social conventions that seemingly cheapen relationships aren't spawning an orgy of responsibility-free canoodling. Instead, young people are opting out. Biologically speaking, this development holds potential long-term consequences for our species.

The inflated sexual assault statistics, muddied language on sex and gender, and hair-trigger extra-judicial punishments combine to create an atmosphere of distrust that further confuses interactions between men and women. That's an amazing feat, by the way. For the entirety of recorded human history, the interactions between men and women have been a source of consternation, confusion, and frustration. Doctoral dissertations, operas, movies, and sitcoms have all explored this mystery, and we are no closer to solving it.

And campus feminists have somehow figured out how to make these interactions more confusing. That's a bona fide achievement.

CHAPTER FIVE

LEFTISM, LIBERALISM, AND LANGUAGE

A year before Dennis was born in Brooklyn, the borough saw an even more famous arrival, Jackie Robinson.

If you're a baseball fan, you know the story: Robinson's 1947 debut with the Brooklyn Dodgers reversed a long-standing, shameful practice in Major League Baseball, the unwritten ban on black ballplayers. Robinson bravely broke that color barrier. MLB re-tells it every April on the anniversary of Robinson's debut, and all thirty major league teams retired Robinson's number.

That's the story we retell every year, right? But it's too simple, according to Dr. Robin DiAngelo.

An education faculty member at the University of Washington, DiAngelo's writings and speeches focus on racial identity politics. In the Jackie Robinson story, she sees an excellent example of how narratives can obscure facts.

"It reinforces this idea that, all by himself, he did something amazing because he was exceptional," DiAngelo observed when we spoke to her for No Safe Spaces. "Now imagine if we told the story like this: Jackie Robinson [was] the first black man that whites allowed to play major league baseball."

That's not a politically correct way to frame the story, to be sure. But, DiAngelo notes, it's probably more accurate. The Dodgers front office (especially general manager Branch Rickey) had to make the first move. They chose and recruited Robinson, and then they decided when he would graduate from the minor leagues and move up to the majors. In fact, Rickey and the Dodgers didn't even choose Robinson to break the color barrier solely based on his baseball acumen; they also factored in his personality, given the resistance they expected from fans and other players.

Truth be told, it was also the deep-abiding Christian faith and moral character of Robinson that made the devoutly Methodist Rickey believe Robinson was the right man to overcome the temptations and obstacles that would be necessary to integrate baseball. According to *Jackie Robinson: A Biography* by Arnold Rampersad, during Rickey's initial meeting with Robinson, he gave the ballplayer a book by Giovanni Papini, titled *Life of Christ*, opening it to the Sermon on the Mount.

This aspect of the history is largely absent from the Hollywood film *42* (the number Robinson wore on his jersey) about Robinson's life. Yet knowing this information changes the story in meaningful ways. For example, knowing that Robinson was chosen—and why he was chosen—actually tells us more about the opposition he faced. It also offers insight into how America struggled with race relations in 1947. The simple narrative of Robinson barging onto the scene just doesn't cut it.

"We have to think critically in the way we tell the story," DiAngelo noted, "because it shapes the way we view the world."

The language we use not only reflects our thoughts, it also helps form them. Different language can expose different facets of reality as it does in the Jackie Robinson story, or it can obscure and confuse.

There are two ways to choke off free expression. We've already discussed one of them: clamp down on free speech and declare some topics off-limits. That strategy is straightforward enough. The other, more insidious way to limit free expression is to try to change the very language people use.

If we're going to talk about language and clarity, we probably ought to be clear about something up front: when we criticize the viewpoint that dominates American college campuses today, we're talking about leftists and not liberals. That's an important distinction.

Adam considers himself a liberal. In fact, many of the people interviewed for No Safe Spaces (people like Greg Lukianoff, Alan Dershowitz, Bret Weinstein, and Dave Rubin) would consider themselves liberals.

It is easy to blame liberal overrepresentation among faculty and administrators for the problems on college campuses. That's worse than an oversimplification. It obscures what's really happening.

"Left" and "liberal" are not the same thing.

Liberals value freedom of speech and freedom of religion. They support due process and equality before the law. They support racial integration. They may want more government involvement in the economy, but they also support capitalism.

Conservatives and liberals may disagree on policy, but they share some basic American values. This gives them common ground for discussion. Conservatives and liberals may engage in heated debates, but having the same foundational values gives them room to compromise. (Note: When Mark's kids were younger, they would ask him, "What are we, Dad? Are we conservative or liberal?" And he would say, "We're anti-stupid." He admits to borrowing that line from a cartoonist named Steve Kelly, but it sums up his political ideology better than the "conservative" label that has recently been assigned to him.)

The Left isn't interested in free discussion. The Left wants people to think and act a certain way, and they are willing to enforce stringent rules to make it happen. They'll highlight racial divisions, rather than work for integration. In their view, individual freedoms take a back seat to enforcing ideas for the common good.

They call this "social justice." That sounds nice, doesn't it? Who could be against justice?

But the language of the Left allows them to push an agenda that doesn't have much in common with liberals or conservatives— or with the Constitution and Declaration of Independence, or

America as it has existed up to now. The Left wants to enforce a notion of "justice" very different from any kind of justice that either conservatives or liberals would recognize.

○⃠

Tricia Beck-Peter admitted her past when we talked to her.

"I was," she confessed, "a social justice warrior."

Since reformed, Beck-Peter now works with the Foundation for Economic Education, an organization dedicated to providing students with the education on free-market capitalism that they might not receive in high school or college.

Like many students, Beck-Peter came to college as a liberal. Her family wasn't particularly political. She fell in with leftists because she thought that was the best way to advance her values.

"I thought that if you thought the gays should be able to get married, and you weren't a racist, you had to be a leftist," Beck-Peter told us. That led her to take some more aggressive stances. "I was an outspoken feminist. I was an outspoken advocate of wealth redistribution. And I was in favor of a lot of censorship for a long time."

Beck-Peter admitted that she used to be one of the people eager to shut down contentious speech. "I thought if anything you said could hurt anybody's feelings," she told us. "It was our job to make you shut up." But she began to see inconsistencies in this line of thought when she ran into someone she and her fellow students called "the Hate Preacher."

(That's a heck of a job title to have on your business card.)

"The Hate Preacher" had a spot on a sidewalk outside the Flagler College library where he would sit and spew hate speech. And we're talking actual, individualized hate speech: He was actively trying to make people feel bad. He would pick fights with passersby, call students vile things, make unwelcome remarks to women, and generally go out of his way to be loud and obnoxious. This was outside the library, so people were going in and out all day and trying to study. Beck-Peter and her friends called the police to no avail: the Hate Preacher's spot on a public sidewalk protected him. Had he stepped on the grass, he would have been trespassing on a private university's property. On the sidewalk, he could say whatever he liked.

At first, Beck-Peter fought to make the sidewalk part of the Flagler College property. This would let the campus police shut Hate Preacher down.

Then she thought about it a little more. She didn't exactly like some of the decisions her college administration made. She might have some things to say about that. If the school could muzzle the Hate Preacher, couldn't they shut down a less hateful, more reasonable protest just as easily?

Beck-Peter found that many other left-wing values shared similarities with the Left's push to limit hate speech: they sounded great, but they were problematic when put into practice.

The Left keeps liberals in the fold by painting conservatives as evil. Sometimes they do it overtly, as when they claim that conservatives are racist, sexist, homophobic, Islamophobic, or whatever other buzzword fits the situation. (Resorting to personal attacks in debates over ideas sounds like the type of tactic that should stop once you outgrow the elementary school playground, but here we are.)

But some of the vilification is more subtle. For example, professors will use terms like "conservative" and "right wing" interchangeably. That very clearly paints a political philosophy that is comfortably within the mainstream of American politics as extreme—especially as they also use "right wing" to describe racist, white nationalist, misogynist, or anti-Semitic groups, thus linking their own conservative political opponents with some of the vilest elements of American discourse.

But left-wingers? They're just "progressives." And who isn't in favor of progress?

⊘

Leftists try to create ambiguity with their use of language, but how they talk speaks volumes about how they think.

For example, consider the 2018 study conducted at the Yale School of Management that looked at how white people conversed with people of color. The study showed that white liberals are more likely to talk down to black people, using simpler words and trying to appear less "competent."

In other words, white liberals are worried about showing up black people.

The arrogance is either maddening or hilarious, or maybe a little of both. Since we're fun, good-natured guys, we'll go with "hilarious."

You have to love the irony. The diversity crowd clamors for equality and representation, but have you actually seen them? They're about as diverse as the checkout line at Whole Foods, and probably loaded with about twice as much quinoa. They rant and rave that we need to take racial representation into everything we do, like they're the great saviors of the forgotten people. And after they tell you how problematic it is that television sitcoms don't have more black, lesbian Muslims in lead roles, this batch of white knights to the rescue will turn around and treat their one token black friend like a child.

What progress!

You want to see their use of language in action? Just wait until next November, when the Christmas season starts up (which will happen before the last piece of Halloween candy gets consumed).

This is a big deal for Dennis. Outside of Jesus and maybe Neil Diamond, there might not have ever been a Jew who loves Christmas as much as Dennis does. When someone wishes him "Happy Holidays," he replies with, "Merry Christmas."

People like to shrug this off and say it isn't a big deal. But saying "Happy Holidays" instead of "Merry Christmas" is actually a pretty big deal. Removing Christmas from the Christmas season is an act of secularization. It's an overt attempt to remove religion from society. (And that's why Dennis stands up for Christmas. You're welcome, Christians. Maybe you can all get together and get him a nice gift. Actually, maybe you should make it eight gifts—one for each day of Hanukkah.)

Another example of language limiting debate can be seen in the Left's substitution of the term "gender" for "sex."

"Sex" used to mean the biological differences between men and women, with genitalia being the most obvious identifier. (We aren't going to go all birds-and-bees on you here. If you aren't hip to the biological differences between men and women, you probably need to go read a more basic book before this one.)

Then the word "gender" became an accepted synonym for "sex". We don't have hard data on this, but the reason must have had something to do with adolescent boys writing "as often as possible" under "sex" when filling out forms. But, however it happened, people began using the word "gender" on things like birth certificates in place of the word "sex."

Then campus activists began talking about "gender" as a function of "social construct." Your gender—in other words, the image that you put out to the world and whether you wear a suit or a dress—became something different from your biological sex.

In our current campus environment, using a pronoun (that is, he or she) that doesn't match someone's "gender identity" can be considered offensive. And not just on campus. In 2016 Canada passed a national law codifying penalties for "mis-gendering" people. Business owners in New York City risk massive fines if they don't call people by their preferred pronouns.

Forbidding "mis-gendering" is just one way the Left seeks to control what we can say—and thus what we think. Another is the hue and cry over "microaggressions." That's what the social justice warriors call elements of everyday life that they claim remind women and minorities of the oppression they are living under. They can be words or phrases, or things even less truly aggressive. For example, a movie with an all-white cast can be a microaggression against racial minorities. Some militant atheists see the motto "In God We Trust" printed on all our money as a microaggression against non-believers.

(By the way, if the U.S. currency in your possession offends you, you can exchange all of it for multiple copies of this book.)

Virtually anything can be a microaggression, and it need not be intentional. Offense is in the eye of the beholder. Forget about banning speech—if anything you say can be a microaggression, you're probably going to keep your yap shut of your own volition.

And that's kind of the point, isn't it?

⊘

Mark's friend Gary Cherone, former lead singer of the rock band Van Halen, once put out an album with his old band Extreme titled "III Sides To Every Story." The three sides are "yours," "mine," and "the truth." Today, apparently there's only one side that matters. The Left's greatest assault on the language may be the phrase "your truth," which has achieved mainstream adoption. Oprah Winfrey uses it, after all. (Forget about the stuffy old *Oxford English Dictionary*. If you want a benchmark for how much cultural *cachet* a phrase has, see how many celebrities use it.)

But what does really it mean to tell "your truth"?

It sounds like an innocuous phrase encouraging people to share their views and experiences, right? Asking people to tell "their truth" just seems like an invitation for them to tell what has happened to them from their perspective. For example, if you want to understand racism in America, you might ask minorities to share their stories.

But look more closely at that phrase: "your truth."

Truth is supposed to be immutable, right? But if someone's experiences are called "their truth," that elevates their opinions from the conditional to the absolute. Their feelings now trump reality.

Really, there is only one "truth." We may ask different people for their views, collect a variety of them, and then be able to extrapolate the truth from that information. But each individual perspective is, by nature, incomplete. *Your* truth is probably not *the* truth.

Let's use a really simple example: Say you want to figure out what color the sky is. You look out your window, and you see a gray, cloudy sky. "Your truth" is that the sky is gray. Let's say you call a few friends. Someone in San Diego says the sky is blue. Someone in Boston sees low, white clouds, so they say it's white. The more people you ask, the more perspectives you get, and the closer you get to figuring out the truth. You might also learn something about weather, so there's a bonus.

Another example might be a girl sharing a story about a time she was treated badly because of her race, sex, sexual orientation, or other characteristic. If you accept this one experience as revelatory of a broad truth about our society, it paints an abysmal picture of America. But instead of making a sweeping generalization based on one experience, she could just chalk it up to running into a jerk—and since we have more than 300 million people in this country, there are going to be a plethora of chances to run into jerks. Like the perspective of Dennis's grandfather, who accused every jackass on the road that didn't even know he was Jewish of acting out of anti-Semitism, this young woman's personal "truth" might need to be modified by other evidence in order for us to arrive at the actual, objective truth about race relations in America.

$\oslash$

Liberals love America. It embodies the basic freedoms that are the underpinnings of conservative and liberal philosophies alike. Free speech, free religion, and free enterprise give us common ground.

Leftists, in contrast, hate America. Everything about it proves their ideology wrong. Capitalism lifts people out of poverty. Speaking the truth and listening to opposing viewpoints, even when it's painful, makes us stronger.

But to advance their agenda, the Left has to shut up opposing opinions and shut out inconvenient facts. Hijacking the language makes that a lot easier.

EXTRA CREDIT: ALAN DERSHOWITZ ON SAFE SPACES

Alan Dershowitz is well known as a criminal defense attorney, a law professor, and an outspoken liberal who had a lot to share about those differences between liberal values and leftism. Here's what he told us:

> Freedom of expression is supposed to protect dissidents, minorities. Now, it depends how you define minority. For example, in the United States of America the intersectionalists, the people who argue that they are the victims, may be a minority; African Americans, gay, lesbian, transgender people, etc. On university campuses, they're not the minority. They're the majority voice, they're the loudest voice. What needs to be protected at university campuses are Zionists, Christians, people who support gun ownership, and indeed people who support free speech, because free speech is an endangered species on university and college campuses today all over the world, not only in the United States.
>
> And, of course, the safe space rationale is a total phony. The last thing that these intersectionalists want to do is

have safe spaces for Jewish Zionists, or for Christians, or for conservatives. They want the university to be unsafe for them, not only intellectually but physically. Whenever I speak on a university campus to make the centrist liberal case for Israel, I need police protection. Nobody wants to give me a safe space. But they demand safe spaces for their ideas. No university should ever create a safe space for an idea. If you want to feel good, get a massage.

If you want to have everybody agreeing with you, join a club, or a group, or a church that agrees with you. But if you want to come to a university you have to be ready to listen to, and express, the most diverse and the most unpopular ideas.

$$\oslash$$

Intersectionalism is a euphemism for anti-Semitism, anti-Christianity. It's simply a way of saying, "We're the victims. We're gays, we're women, we're blacks, and we all have the same oppressors. Our oppressors are the Zionists, the United States of America, capitalists, imperialists. We're the victims, and we have to hang together, and we need safe spaces, but we're not going to give you any safe spaces because you really have no right to express your views." That's the basic core belief of the hard Left on American campuses today—and they'll tell it to you directly, that certain views should not be allowed to be expressed on campus.

I grew up during the McCarthy period when it was the extreme Right at Brooklyn College which told me I had no right to express my views, and it was the liberals who were demanding free speech, and the conservatives who were trying to deny it. Today it's flipped, and it's the extreme Left that is denying free speech not only to conservatives but to liberals. Remember, liberals are the arch-enemies of the radicals, just like conservatives are the arch-enemies of the extreme Right.

⊘

You know, it's hard because if you're a liberal like me, you're attacked repeatedly by both sides. I have a thick skin. I grew up as a criminal defense attorney. But you should read my emails from both the hard Left, which regard me as a complete traitor to the Left, and by the hard Right, which regard liberalism as the same as radicalism. So I get it from both sides. Look, I thrive on controversy. Many people don't, and they shrink from taking the liberal position. Look, liberalism is dying in America. It's so hard to find real liberalism. I remember my debates with Bill Buckley. We could have a true conservative and a true liberal, we both agreed on freedom of speech, and we would have disagreements that were interesting.

⊘

The hard Left poses a far greater danger to the American future than the hard Right. I'm not worried about a few dozen people with swastikas who want to replace the Jews, because they're our past. They have no residence on university campuses today. But the hard Left, anti-Semitism, anti-Christianity, intolerance for speech, it's the future. These are our leaders.

When I used to teach 150 students in my first year of criminal law I'd look around, and I'd say future president, future chief justice, future editorial director of the *New York Times*, future managing partner of Goldman Sachs. They're our future, and that's why we have to worry much more about what's going on [at] university campuses than in Charlottesville.

◌

I've lost a little weight because I wasn't invited to dinner parties on Martha's Vineyard this summer very often. I'm getting different kinds of invitations to speak. People confuse my views with jumping ship, leaving the liberals, and somehow becoming conservative or right wing, because it's very hard for people to understand the true liberal philosophy. Now, "liberal" can be a political conservative or a political progressive. Liberal values have to do with the nature of the dialogue, the nature of the exchange of views.

◌

Many on the left love hate speech if it's directed against Jews, against Israel, against Christians, against conservatives.

That's their *modus operandi*, hate speech. But if it's directed against them, even if it's minimally critical, it's hate speech, it's white supremacy, the new code word. If you say anything controversial, you're a white supremacist, you're a sexist, you're anti-Muslim, and you're homophobic.

CHAPTER SIX

ACADEMIC FAILURE

The history of the Soviet Union may seem like an odd topic to mull over in a psychology classroom. However, if you find yourself taking Jordan Peterson's second-year Personality Psychology class at the University of Toronto, you might hear some things you've never heard before.

Peterson told Adam that although most of the students in his classroom are well-educated and even lean toward the conservative side of the political aisle, they "don't know a damn thing about what happened in the Soviet Union."

That speaks volumes about what passes for "well-educated" these days.

Most of us remember the Soviet Union as America's Cold War rival. For about fifty years after the end of World War II, the planet was divided between allies of the Union of Soviet Socialist Republics (U.S.S.R.) and allies of the United States of America (U.S.A.). Neutral countries, or countries whose allegiance hung in the balance (places like Korea, Vietnam, and Grenada), were thankfully the only major spots where the ideological conflict flared into actual combat. The two rival powers did come close to war a few times, most famously and publicly during the Cuban Missile Crisis of 1962.

For those with no memory of the Cold War, the bitter rivalry was the geopolitical equivalent of the Boston Celtics versus the Los Angeles Lakers, or the New York Yankees versus the Boston Red Sox: two evenly matched, powerful entities vying for dominance. Adam's mother would tell him that for every American worried about the Soviets, some Soviet family was just as fearful of the Americans (and that they were equally justified for feeling that way).

As Peterson teaches, history has proven that this idea was completely and utterly wrong.

The Communist ideology dreamed up by Karl Marx in nineteenth-century Germany, which formed the foundation for the Soviet Union and other regimes, led to millions of murders during (and before) the Cold War—estimates put the actual count somewhere in the neighborhood of 20 to 60 million people, depending on who is tallying corpses in the mass graves. Marxist nations had to put up walls and severely restrict travel—not to keep people out, but to prevent people from defecting. Post-war America enjoyed a capitalism-fueled economic boom that raised the standard of living to the point where even working class people could own things like cars and televisions. In Communist countries, the poor had to stand in line for things like bread and toilet paper. (Though records are scarce, we can be relatively certain it was single-ply toilet paper.) Even those who are aware of the Soviet Union's various purges and atrocities may have heard them blamed on a bastardized version of Marxism implemented by Vladimir Lenin or Josef Stalin.

History shows us that isn't true. Wherever Marx's ideas are implemented, the results are the same: poverty, repression, and murder. But those facts haven't been communicated to many of the students in Peterson's lecture halls.

"They've never been taught any of that," he said incredulously.

Peterson pointed out that Marxist philosophy creates a dichotomy between an oppressor class and an oppressed class. The Communists built economic theory on that idea—everyone was either a rich Daddy Warbucks or a poor Orphan Annie—and they thought the government's main role was to redistribute wealth from the rich to the poor. The identity politics of today's campuses follow that pattern, too. "Cultural Marxism" creates the same dichotomy between oppressor and oppressed, between the privileged classes and the protected classes.

Now you might ask why supposedly smart academics would bank on an ideology that has failed every time it has been tried and resulted in tens of millions of deaths.

It is because this time—*this time*—they're sure Marxism is going to work!

If you go to a nutritionist looking to lose weight, you pretty much know the response you're going to get: Eat more vegetables. Stay away from carbs and sugar. Exercise more. Eat broccoli. Do push-ups.

Why? Because scientifically, we know that these habits lead to weight loss. We know the chemical processes within the body that burn calories, and we have seen healthy diet and exercise work before. The theory is sound. The practice is sound.

Now imagine there's one nutritionist going around telling people that the information isn't accurate. Instead, they're telling people whatever they want to hear. "Go ahead and chow down on carbs and candy bars," this hypothetical nutritionist might say. "Consume as much pizza and pasta as you can. Watch at least seven hours of television each day. Take plenty of naps."

"Carbs and couch sitting won't necessarily make you fat," this nutritionist would add. "It just hasn't been tried the right way yet. If you chow down on doughnuts by the dozen and sit on the lounge the right way, you'll be fine!"

Now imagine everyone starts following this nutritionist's advice, believing that carbs and naps will lead to good health. And every person on the doughnut-and-doze plan is packing on pounds like a late-stage Elvis impersonator trying to make weight for an off-strip Vegas show. Doughnuts are delicious, and naps are refreshing. People are less healthy and feeling more and more like a deflated car tire, but the only solution offered is another nap or more dessert. And the person who pipes up and suggests, "Hey, maybe roll off the couch and try to do a sit-up?" gets lambasted for being culturally insensitive.

Out on the *No Safe Spaces* tour, we have seen campus after campus infected with a political culture that's just as toxic. It would be bad enough if the problem were just emanating from the administration building. But sadly, the toxicity comes from (and gets reinforced in) the classroom. Like our rogue nutritionist, professors have adopted feel-good cultural Marxism at the expense of the university's educational mission.

Professors aren't doing their jobs. The obvious effect: dumber college graduates.

Maybe calling them dumb is too harsh; let's call them "less educated." Any way you slice it, the truth is that American college graduates know embarrassingly little about the society in which they live. A 2015 survey by the American Council of Trustees and Alumni (ACTA) showed that college graduates have no idea about basic concepts of American government. More than half (60 percent) of the grads surveyed didn't know how amendments to the U.S. Constitution get ratified. Nearly half didn't know how long Congressional terms of office are. About one out of ten people surveyed thought Judge Judy was on the Supreme Court. Perhaps they thought she was nominated to fill the vacancy left by Judge Wapner (may he rest in peace).

(That last statistic sounds like it's a joke Adam sneaked into the book, doesn't it? Nope.)

ACTA has been surveying Americans' historic and civic knowledge for a number of years. In recent years they have found that one third of those surveyed didn't know Franklin Delano Roosevelt gave us the New Deal, fewer than half identified George Washington as the general in the decisive battle of the American Revolution, and fewer than a third could place the Civil War within the correct twenty-year time period.

Since America's founding, few events have shaped national history like the Civil War. And one out of three college graduates can't place it within twenty years? You could chuck darts at a timeline while blindfolded and get within twenty years of the Civil War.

The Intercollegiate Studies Institute also found broad problems with Americans' civic knowledge: 71 percent of Americans surveyed in their 2008 study would fail a basic history test. (And fewer than 50 percent could even name all three branches of government.)

The problem is not limited to history or political science departments.

In 2016, students at the Ivy League University of Pennsylvania took down a portrait of William Shakespeare that had hung in the English Department's building and replaced it with a picture of Audre Lorde, a black female poet and activist whose writings became increasingly left-wing throughout the 1970s. Penn, like most of America's top-ranked universities, does not require English majors to take courses in Shakespeare.

The downfall of Shakespeare at Penn and other campuses comes as literary professors seek to add more diverse options to the English canon. There is obvious value in including different voices; but there is obvious harm in excluding voices, too. Not only are Shakespeare's works on the short list of the greatest literature in our language, they have shaped the English we speak and the world's entertainment for the past four hundred years. Understanding Shakespeare will help students understand a lot of their own experiences. (Have you ever seen Disney's *The Lion King*? It's essentially *Hamlet* with a mane.)

Great works are great works partly because they're a solid foundation on which a lot of other culture is built. Imagine trying to build a house without a foundation. Sure, you might get it built, and it might even look nice, but it would be very easy for it to tip over in the slightest breeze.

Shakespeare was among the first literary masters who was able to create great literature with popular appeal. Writing at a time when non-aristocrats were largely illiterate, Shakespeare was able to make his writing transcend that boundary using the stage. Shakespeare's plays were the equivalent of movie adaptations. He even invented words and phrases that we still use today: *eventful, fashionable, pageantry,* and *bedazzled* all come from Shakespeare's plays. (That's right: the people who created the "Bedazzler"—the infomercial product that lets you add rhinestones to any article of clothing you own—can say their work was inspired by Shakespeare.)

This isn't meant to denigrate Lorde or her work. But if you want an understanding of the English language and its literature, you can get by without reading Lorde. You cannot get by without knowing Shakespeare.

Let's put it another way: If you were teaching twentieth-century American poetry, you might want to include Lorde. She was a prominent voice in both the feminist and black power movements, so that's a natural fit. You certainly wouldn't drop her work from the course to include Shakespeare in the interest of including more white men, right?

Professors have looked at their classrooms and seen political activists in training, rather than citizens in training. They have quit teaching how our institutions work and imparting history's significant facts. They choose the literature they teach based on what the author looks like.

Meanwhile, there are more college graduates in our population than we've ever had before.

According to a 2017 report by the U.S. Census Bureau, one out of three American adults (33.4 percent) over the age of twenty-five has a four-year college degree.[1] That's up from 28 percent in 2007. When the census bureau first asked the education question in 1940, only 4.6 percent reported having a bachelor's degree. The GI Bill, which helped send servicemembers coming back from World War II to college, and explosions in Pell Grants and other financial aid programs made college more accessible. (They also made college more expensive—more on that later.)

But while we are getting more educated, we are not getting smarter.

Jordan Peterson also worries about the long-term effects of students' deficient education on their states of mind. (Which, given his field of study, makes sense.)

"I think the humanities in particular have become corrupt to the point of presenting a credible social danger," Peterson warned. "They undermine the psychological health of their students."

Peterson worries that professors, by reinforcing identity politics and victimhood status, are giving students every reason to be as miserable as a rabbit being stalked by a wolf.

"If you're a victim surrounded by predators—by evil predators—you're frozen," Peterson explained. "If you think of any animal in a situation like that, the animal's frozen in terror, right?"

College is supposed to be the best time of your life. Instead, students get to hear that they are oppressed (or, conversely, that their very existence oppresses someone else). Imagine hearing that in class after class, up and down your academic schedule. Imagine having to write paper after paper—five pages, ten pages, a senior thesis—detailing how life gave you a raw deal (or how you made other people's lives a living hell just by taking your first breath). Class after class, year after year, for four years.

What these students are really hearing is that society is built for them to fail.

If you've ever been to a carnival, you've seen rigged games before—like one of those basketball games where the hoop is only a little bit bigger than the ball, so you have to make the shot just right for the ball to go in. That is the picture of life that professors are presenting to their students. Life is a rigged carnival game: you have to be lucky and perfect, or you will lose, and some travelling grifter will take all your money.

When you see a game like that, you probably keep walking down the concourse in search of a funnel cake. And that's the lesson students are hearing: Keep walking. Don't play. Do take in something that's delicious and satisfying but altogether unhealthy. The fix is in, so you can't win. Don't bother working hard or trying to better yourself, because systemic oppression—it's built right into the system!—will hold you down. The people sitting at the top of the power structure are there only because of the inherited advantages of their skin color, gender, or class—there's no hard work or talent involved.

But here's the thing: That's obviously untrue. We've seen enough determined, hard-working people succeed—despite race, gender, class, sexual orientation, or physical or mental disability. The success stories are all around us. The evidence is as clear as the sky is blue.

On top of colleges not teaching basic facts to make us smarter, they are actively sabotaging new grads by sending them into the workforce with encouragement *not* to do the things that lead to success: work hard, build a family, and cultivate a positive attitude.

College classrooms actively sabotage our graduates.

Why do professors do this? Why do they hold their cultural Marxism in such high esteem that they ignore the evidence and set their charges off on such a destructive path?

Envy probably has something to do with it.

If you're a college professor, it means years of education in addition to the basic twelve to sixteen years suffered by everyone else. That additional schooling doesn't necessarily make you smarter, but it does make you more educated; plus, it means you probably have some level of passion for a given field of study. For all your hard work, though, you're sitting in front of a classroom, lecturing a roomful of kids. Half of them probably look like they don't want to be there, and few of them will care about your subject matter even a quarter as much as you do.

If that isn't frustrating enough, you look (sometimes longingly) at the corporate world. Maybe some of your buddies from undergrad ended up there after they got their business degrees. People who are no smarter than you (and probably quite a few who aren't as smart) are making more money, living in bigger houses, and driving fancier cars.

Of course, you're a Marxist, so such things aren't important to you. It still irks you, though, that you're driving to campus in a Toyota while your freshman-year roommate tools around in a Lexus. How do you justify the difference?

You could discuss how great it is that in America people can choose their own status symbols and decide what makes them happy. You might enumerate the rewards you get from being an educator and explain how that affects your happiness. You could reassure your students that you are comfortable with your decision to trade a higher income in the corporate world for the opportunities you have enjoyed.

Alternatively, you could fall into the nice, comfortable hammock of claiming the system is rigged.

This mindset absolves the professor from any blame for his socio-economic status, just as it absolves his students of taking responsibility for their own lives. But who's blaming the professor in the first place? No one. The professor projects all his own baggage onto his class. (Jordan Peterson could have a field day with this hypothetical professor, couldn't he?)

University faculty enjoy a relatively safe existence, especially once they achieve tenure.

That's a feature, not a bug. Peterson told Adam he views the professorial life as a trade-off. "You're supposed to be offered security so that you will take intellectual risks," said Peterson. "That's the bargain."

The idea is that by taking those academic risks, professors can expand minds and (even if they offend a few people) offer genuinely mind-stretching discussions. The university is supposed to protect this freedom for its faculty. (Maybe that's where the idea of the ivory tower comes from—you need a place to hide from the hordes of people you might offend.)

But Peterson pointed out that professors sometimes play it safe. "You can get the security and then not take intellectual risks or any kind of risk at all."

Security breeds complacency, and it's the kind of complacency you might not even notice. Professors can feel avant-garde writing and lecturing about ideas that are outside the mainstream of American society, or promoting concepts that would radically upend our economic system. But how edgy are you in an environment where everyone is trying to do the same thing? When a professor goes on a tirade about white privilege or toxic masculinity, are other professors going to protest? Nope. The only conflict will be about who gets to be first in line to say congratulations and reverently tell the professor how "brave" he or she was. Be careful way out there on that limb, Professor Plum.

When a college hires a professor, it isn't hiring a mere instructor, either. "Professor" is not synonymous with "teacher." A university professor must also demonstrate his or her worth through research and publications. You may have heard the old saying "publish or perish." This means that if a professor is not getting books, research papers, and other writings in print, his job is in peril. A lecture hall of a hundred students could spend a semester becoming geniuses, but the professor's job security doesn't really improve because of it. The focus on publications and research tells the professor that his or her job is really to satisfy other academics.

Those other academics aren't the ones who bankroll the whole academic enterprise. That instead falls to the students (which means the parents of those students, in most cases). Regardless of who is actually signing the checks, they're paying more each year: In 2017, the College Board reported that over just thirty years, per-year tuition at private four-year schools has more than doubled, even after adjusting for inflation. At public four-year institutions, average tuition costs have more than tripled.

(By the way, after you finish college, they still like to call you and ask for donations—though as Adam frequently points out, the Ditch Digger University fundraising program remains delightfully unobtrusive.)

And when students can't pay out of pocket, they are turning to that tried-and-true American funding source: Faustian levels of debt. Seven out of every ten graduates have gone into debt to fund their undergraduate educations,[2] and the United States collectively owes about $1.5 trillion in student loans.[3] The tricky thing about student loans: they stay with the students. As soon as the dean hands you your diploma, you're suddenly on the hook for a significant chunk of money.

Much like the since-popped housing bubble of the mid-2000s, this loan debt also has government fingerprints all over it. For the 2016–2017 school year, the federal government spent $239 billion on higher education, according to data collected by the College Board. That included almost $95 billion on federally backed student loans. Students took out close to $12 billion more in nonfederal student loans.[4]

And like anything else that gets subsidized, the more tax dollars headed to colleges and universities, the more expensive they became. What the government thinks of as "aid," college administrators think of as "new revenue."

In 1988, when tuition at the average private four-year college was $17,000 per year, there was no "student shortage" in higher education.[5] There weren't piles of books sitting on unused desks, collecting dust in the corners of deserted classrooms. Colleges and universities were doing just fine. But politicians thought it would be good if more people could go to college, so they voted to fund new programs, created new grants, allowed access to more loans, and increased students' purchasing power.

The idea was that these subsidies would give people more financial flexibility. Kids whose parents hadn't been able to save could now afford the tuition. And maybe the money parents had managed to save for their kids' college costs could go to other things. That is an admirable goal, but it's just totally divorced from reality.

You know what colleges did when people got more money to spend on education? Raised tuition. They didn't care if the money was coming from a student's pocket, or Uncle Sam's, or both. It's simple supply and demand. (We really can't understand how the Marxists are missing this.)

And it's not just the taxpayers who are getting bilked. Lots of patriotic conservative Americans are giving millions of dollars to their alma maters, essentially helping to subsidize left-wing indoctrination on college campuses. If they think their money is going to buy them indulgences, they are sorely mistaken. This is sort of like feeding an alligator, hoping he will eat you last.

Nineteen-fifties crooner Pat Boone has given millions to Pepperdine University, whose Malibu campus, after months of protests, recently removed a statue of Columbus. How long is it going to take to scrub Boone's name from Pepperdine's "Boone Center for the Family" once leftist students hear the unfair accusations of racism against him (he recorded songs by African-American artists and questioned the location of President Obama's birth)? Nothing's gonna change until rich alumni quit writing checks to their old schools like it's still 1952.

Colleges and universities solicit these huge donations and charge these exorbitant sums under the pretense that they provide an environment that offers an opportunity for intellectual enrichment. They justify it by talking about how high school graduates need four years of post-secondary education to function in civilized society.

For too many academic institutions, that has become a fraudulent claim.

You can't just shrug your shoulders and say, "Buyer beware!" The taxpayers are on the hook, too. We shovel billions in state and federal tax dollars for student aid (on top of the funding that state schools get from state taxpayers) onto the dumpster fire that is higher education today.

With as much money as colleges ask for—and get—it's fair to ask if students are getting their money's worth.

$\oslash$

For a few generations of guidance counselors, higher education provided an easy answer when high school seniors asked, "What should I do next?"

In addition to that, movies like *Animal House*, *Back to School*, *PCU*, and *Division III: Football's Finest* have romanticized the college experience a bit. College looks like a fun place to be for four years while you procrastinate getting a job.

So we all have the idea that everyone needs to go to some sort of college after high school. Someone with only a high school diploma now is viewed the same way a high school dropout might have been viewed thirty or forty years ago. And our policies and our advice to high school students orient them in that direction. We subsidize college with government money, and we encourage every student to go to college.

What about people who don't need college?

Does the person fixing your sink need a college education? Do you care how he did in "English 145: Voices of Queer Black Literature, 1946–1953" during his freshman year? Nope. You just need someone who can unclog the drain and won't gouge you on the price.

How does the guy doing your drywall feel about intersectional feminist theory? What is your airline pilot's policy regarding reparations for the descendants of American slaves? Which beat poet does your roofer think was the most influential?

Undergraduate education tries to answer these questions, which are some of the least-relevant questions you could ask of any of these tradesmen. You want your drywall to stay up, you want your plane to land intact, and you want your roof to stop leaking. That's all you care about, and you're willing to pay for it. If people are interested in things like beat poetry or Queer Black Literature from 1946 to 1953, nothing will stop them from pursuing that subject. It has never been easier to find resources to learn more and connect with others who have shared interests. There is a Facebook page or group out there for just about anything, and that's just the tip of the Internet iceberg.

(It is also worth noting that a college dropout started Facebook. Same with Microsoft. Just think how much more successful Mark Zuckerberg and Bill Gates could be with college degrees. That probably keeps them up at night.)

With traditional schools failing to adequately educate and prepare students, the American free market has stepped in to some degree. In the early-to-mid-2000s, for-profit schools (such as the University of

Phoenix and Strayer University) grew, as advancements in technology made it easier for them to offer (and easier for students to take) online courses. Traditional brick-and-mortar schools and their cheerleaders (metaphorical cheerleaders, not the people on the sideline at football games) flipped out, calling these entities diploma mills. (Now more and more traditional schools are pushing their *own* online education programs using the same basic model.)

The non-profit education sector had allies in then President Barack Obama's Department of Education and Consumer Financial Protection Bureau, which used regulatory burdens to limit students' ability to use financial aid at these institutions. The government's stated concern was that for-profit institutions would lure students with unfulfilled promises and leave them struggling with debt. If that sounds familiar, it's because that's what non-profit colleges and universities have done for decades. They offer a sub-par education as it applies to the real world, and they have priced out many who either don't qualify for subsidies or who don't care to start their careers lugging around a boulder of debt.

As a side note, you have to admire the gall of traditional educational institutions calling themselves "non-profit." Yes, it's a legal definition, since they accept donations that are tax-deductible. But for schools like Harvard University—which charges $67,000 a year in tuition, fees, and room and board, and has an endowment of $37 billion—to call itself a "non-profit" with a straight face is, on some level, utterly hilarious. Among the profiters (or is it profiteers?) are the college administrators. According to the *Chronicle of Higher Education*'s eighth annual survey of public university presidents' compensation, James Ramsey of the University of Louisville made $4.3 million in 2017. Jay Gogue of Auburn University, who made around $2.5 million, came in a distant second (still, it's hard to feel sorry for him). But even the heads of private Christian schools are raking in the big bucks. Azusa Pacific University, for example, pays their president, Jon Wallace, a whopping $382,270 (when you factor in things like nontaxable benefits).

While for-profit entities struggle to rebound from their regulatory fights, "bootcamps" have risen to partially supplant them. As their name implies, bootcamps are short, focused educational programs that teach a certain skill, such as computer programming. If you're interested, you'd better find a bootcamp soon, because those will no doubt get shut down (probably about three weeks before Cornell University starts advertising an online coding bootcamp on billboards in Texas, or South Carolina, or somewhere else far from Ithaca, New York).

Instead of thinking about the role of vocational and technical education, or giving people the real tools to make a living and excel in life, we're stuffing eighteen-year-olds into a lecture hall, telling half of them they'll never succeed in life, and telling the other half that it's all their fault.

It is such a load of crap that you have to wonder how a toilet ever gets unclogged in this country.

EXTRA CREDIT: COLLEEN SHEEHAN ON ACADEMIA

Colleen Sheehan is a professor of political science at Villanova University. There, she serves as the director of the Matthew J. Ryan Center for the Study of Free Institutions and the Public Good. Here's what she told us about the current state of academia:

> A free society takes risks. And we have to not be afraid of those risks. We have to embrace them and follow the

arguments. That's where liberal education and the conditions of a free society sort of come together. Both involve dangers. But those dangers are part of the human condition. And if they're dealt with, we have a much better chance of guarding against them than if we ignore them, put them away, and try to provide protections that end up really just abdicating our responsibilities to deal with the questions.

This idea of safe spaces in which you're protected against hearing things that you don't like, that you find offensive—and of course, lots of things can be offensive to lots of people…. I'm all for protecting our young folks, but I'm not sure that that's the way to do it. That's coddling that protects them while they're in this kind of environment, which some people call the bubble of the university.

But there is a real world out there, and the real world involves all kinds of challenges in which people have to be able to stand up for themselves and do it with dignity and with knowledge—full knowledge—of why their views and their actions deserve to be respected, and why they should respect the views and actions of others. And what happens with this kind of coddling in safe spaces is an abdication of any kind of responsibility for dealing with these kinds of issues.

And that leads to…a paternalism which keeps these kids as kids all their lives, rather than allowing them to grow up and to be full and flourishing human beings, and to take upon themselves the responsibilities that go along with being adults.

Universities across America are in a position where they're not sure of who they are anymore. The meaning of the university was to come together, to search for truth.... And so all kinds of different opinions and approaches and conclusions were part of university life.

Today, many folks at the university seem to either be afraid of that pursuit or just not to like it, to reject it—which means rejecting the mission of the university. It also means rejecting doing our job as professors, putting these questions on the table for the students, for the young people, and engaging them in this search for the truth.

When you cut that off, what the university becomes is more of a place to preach to people a certain set of ideas that are acceptable in a very narrow framework. It's somewhat akin to despotism, in which you decide there's a party line, and only those kinds of things can be spoken and promoted. There are all kinds of questions that are off limits, all kinds of discussions that are off limits.

Whatever that is, that is not a genuine university.

$$\oslash$$

Some of the folks who are imposing those kinds of rules, trying to limit speech and so on, many of them have good intentions.

They care about others. They don't want young people to feel uncomfortable, to feel hurt by criticisms, particularly criticisms about things that they have no responsibility for: race, economic level, sex, and so on. The things that they don't choose but are a part of who they are. That's under-standable.

But that shouldn't lead to coddling and to limiting speech. We should talk about these things. We should be courageous enough to think that maybe there is an answer that's a good answer, and that we don't have to hide from it.

○

It's a question for each of us in every single generation. Do we want our lives to be our own or do we want them to belong to someone else, essentially? The baby boomers and the millennials aren't totally different in this regard. Each one has the same challenge: the challenge of living up to the standards of our humanity....

It's always a challenge for human beings to live—not just to live their lives, not just to exist—but to live their lives with dignity. And that's a challenge for all young people today.

But to do that, they've got to stand up for themselves. They've got to have ideas. As Robert Frost once said, ideas aren't things just to learn in college and then put away. They're things to knit about, to pick up every so often. The good ones. The important ones. You've got to pick them up every so often and knit about them.... We don't want to just have mere opinions about things. We want to have thoughts about things. That's what it means to be educated. That's what it means to be human. That's our challenge as professors, not to tell students what to think, but to get them to think, and for them to make their ideas and their beliefs fully their own. Yes, that's a challenge for young people today. It's a challenge for human beings everywhere and at all times.

CHAPTER SEVEN

UNSAFE SPACES

I n the late Middle Ages, Jews found themselves unwelcome in Portugal and Spain. Not unwelcome in the "tough-to-get-a-table-or-catch-a-cab" way. This was the "forced-conversion-or-die" level of unwelcome, going back at least to the 1300s. In 1492, all Jews who did not convert to Christianity were expelled from Spain. And Portugal's original edict of expulsion of 1496 was turned into an edict of forced conversion in 1497.

Many Jews converted, left, or were simply massacred. Some Spanish Jews opted to hide their Judaism, pretending to be Catholic while practicing their true faith in secret to avoid punishment. They became known as "Marranos."

Of course, colleges and universities today do not oppress conservatives as severely as the regimes of the late-medieval Iberian peninsula oppressed Jews. But the analogy of Marranos—people who hide their true views in order not to be hurt in some way—is instructive. For many students, holding center-right—or even, really, commonsense—viewpoints and ideas can be very troublesome. Many conservatives feel that they have to hide their beliefs, like the Marranos, in order to get through four years and earn their degrees without incident.

The term "safe spaces" suggests areas where people can feel secure that they won't be attacked for who they are. But it turns out that the people banging the drum for inclusion, tolerance, and diversity have conditions. They want to make sure everyone has a voice—just so long as everyone uses that voice to say the same thing.

If you challenge their orthodoxy, you're going to be in some sort of trouble. It might take the form of a failing grade, or perhaps social exclusion by the people you thought were your friends. In some cases, it might get even worse. (And if you're in some protected class and you speak out, you will be a special target.)

As colleges and universities became dominated by the Left, tolerance and diversity fell by the wayside. The rising hostility toward liberal values like free speech has made entire college campuses *un*safe spaces for people who align with the Right.

Kingsborough Community College is one of the twenty campuses that make up the City University of New York. Altogether, CUNY boasts a total enrollment of about 274,000 students.

Michael Goldstein, a business communications professor at Kingsborough, has advice for any of those 274,000 who count themselves as conservative: "Don't talk. Keep your mouth shut."

Goldstein isn't issuing that as a threat, but a warning. It's not the advice we would give, but Goldstein doesn't offer it lightly: he has watched left-wing ideology overrun his own campus, and he sees a dead end for any student or aspiring faculty member who steps out of line.

"The classrooms are huge echo chambers where they congratulate themselves on who can be more progressive," Goldstein told us. And it's not limited to political science or social justice classes, either. Political concerns are creeping into departments as far-flung as business and culinary arts.

Goldstein fears this has created a chilling effect for faculty and students. Some students, he noted, have passed up extracurricular opportunities because they felt ostracized socially. As for himself and the handful of right-leaning faculty, "We kind of exchange knowing glances as if we were gay men in the 1950s."

Conservative professors, Goldstein explained, have little chance of being hired at CUNY if their viewpoints are known in advance. That is part of a self-promulgating system, he said, as programs are overtly built not only to educate but also to indoctrinate—especially courses of study designed to produce the next generation of faculty.

"The progressive faculty at this university say each and every day, 'We are not training students here; we are training people who are activists for a progressive agenda.'"

Goldstein explained, "Academia has become a conservative-free zone."

Tyler Brandt discovered that early on at the University of Wisconsin.

Like many of his fellow students, Brandt spent some of his time in Madison as an activist. The school has an active political scene, and it doesn't hurt that the campus is just a few miles from the Wisconsin state house. (Back in 2011, you may remember organized labor holding college-style sit-ins at the state capitol, protesting cuts in state funding during a budget crisis.) But unlike most of UW's activists, Brandt advocated for more conservative beliefs. He chaired his campus chapter of the libertarian-leaning Young Americans for Liberty.

But when he stepped into his first political science class, he found the marketplace of ideas had narrowed a bit.

"We were supposed to write a movie review, or a book review, or a poem review, and then apply the law to that situation," recalled Brandt. He chose Quentin Tarantino's *The Hateful Eight*. On his first pass, he wrote about the frontier law meted out in the movie, and how not every disagreement or dispute needs to be solved by the government.

If you choose a Tarantino movie for a project in your poli-sci course, you might expect to hear a few four-letter f-words, but Brandt probably wasn't expecting to hear this one from his instructor: "Fail."

"It was the first time I've ever gotten an 'F' in my life," says Brandt. The instructor told him to rewrite and resubmit the paper.

So Brandt took another crack. This time, instead of a libertarian take, his paper explored social justice themes and the legacy of slavery. And surprise! That went over better than the previous version.

"I ended up getting an 'A' on it," says Brandt. "That tells you enough about the kind of stuff you have to do at that school."

Over his four years at Wisconsin, Brandt saw the same script play out for his peers, most of whom didn't even share his activist streak.

"I had so many friends who were pretty much apolitical for the most part," recalls Brandt. But social justice themes and ideas permeated "every single department, every single corner of the university."

He saw the same thing during a classroom debate in a philosophy course. The discussion was supposed to be an exercise in applying logic to ethical questions.

The topic of the day was whether all lives could be considered equally valuable. Brandt argued that, though the claim that all lives are equally valid "sounds good socially," if Mahatma Gandhi's life was more valuable than Adolph Hitler's life, then the answer had to be "no."

The philosophy professor said Brandt was being *too* logical—that he should think "more humanistically." This is like a math professor wondering if two plus two always has to equal four, or a geography professor asking a student to reconsider calling Madagascar an island.

Brandt found himself going outside the classroom to round out his education. He consulted online resources from think tanks to find the viewpoints his professors couldn't or wouldn't give in the classroom. (Imagine paying all that money to go to a school, and you have to go and do your own research because they're only giving you half of an education. That's like showing up at Denny's for a Grand Slam breakfast and being told, "You have to go find a chicken if you want us to give you eggs.")

As someone plugged into national groups like Young Americans for Liberty, Brandt knew where to look for those resources. But it wasn't so easy for some of his peers.

"The majority of people just give in."

⊘

At Cornell University, Olivia Corn tried to balance things out when she chaired the College Republicans organization. To let students hear other viewpoints, she and her group invited speakers to campus.

The university was happy to oblige, of course—though they asked the College Republicans to cover the security costs.

Three weeks after the 2016 Presidential election, Corn and the College Republicans hosted former Senator Rick Santorum. The shouting—much of it directed at her—started as soon as Corn tried to introduce Santorum. They called her sexist, a racist, a bigot, and she recalls someone yelling that she was a "disgrace to women." When Santorum launched into his speech, fifty hecklers stood up and shouted over him.

Corn turned to the administration-mandated security guards, who were costing her organization $5,000. "Can we remove these people?" she asked of the hecklers disrupting the event. The security guards said they couldn't remove anyone who wasn't breaking the law.

That $5,000 comes on top of speaking fees, by the way. Conservative speakers don't just show up on college campuses. When student groups bring speakers, they have to shell out thousands of dollars, which means they have to undertake an extensive fundraising effort. (Organizations like Young America's Foundation provide considerable help, but even then it's up to students to make up any difference.) So having Rick Santorum come to speak took considerable effort and hard work. The $5,000 security payment to the university should have ensured that the event was able to happen, right? But apparently it worked more like some kind of Mafia protection racket, where the $5,000 doesn't really protect anything, and then the muscle comes back looking for more money.

On that note: when the College Republicans invited former House Speaker Newt Gingrich later that year, it cost them another *$5,000* in security fees.

With help from a reporter for a campus newspaper, and after some digging, Corn found that her counterparts in the Cornell Democrats had not been asked to pay a dime in security fees for any of their speakers.

Corn shared another story about speakers at Cornell, and it's both funny and sad. When the non-partisan Cornell Political Union invited a conservative speaker who had been active in the Tea Party, they faced the same requirement to pay heavy security costs. But that organization, which brings in multiple speakers from across the political spectrum, couldn't afford the security measures. The alternative was to make it a private event for club members only. The protesters whose bad behavior necessitated the security in the first place then protested the fact that the event was closed.

Columbia University, Cornell's fellow Ivy League institution, has a rule: if a guest speaker comes to campus, heckling is not allowed.

(And Barnard College, the independent women's college that shares many resources and facilities with Columbia, shares that rule as well.) Everyone's right to speak is protected—on paper.

"On paper" is the operative phrase, as Morgan Realm found out.

In her third year at Barnard, Realm participated in Republican, libertarian, and pro-Israel student groups. Her pro-Israel group invited Israeli ambassador Danny Danon, only to watch him get shouted down by coordinated protests; each time security escorted one group of hecklers to the exits, another would spring up to take their place.

It was even worse for Tommy Robinson, the British hard-right activist with a reputation for anti-Muslim comments. By the time Robinson came to speak on European immigration, Columbia was no stranger to controversial speakers; remember that they had previously welcomed former Iranian President Mahmoud Ahmadinejad to speak from a Columbia-sanctioned lectern.

Robinson spoke from a screen via Skype. Realm recalls that protesters surrounded the screen, shouting at Robinson and refusing to give any of the audience members unobstructed views.

Since Robinson couldn't get a word in edgewise, they moved to a question and answer session. Then the hecklers turned on the questioners.

"Even the people [who] were asking questions—you know, real discussion questions, trying to challenge him, even they were shouted down," Realm recalled.

This time, no one was escorted away. The policy against heckling wasn't worth the paper it was printed on. When Columbia opened an investigation and suggested they were thinking about enforcing the rule, a faculty petition insisted that the protesters should be absolved and the matter should be dropped.

Predictably, Columbia acquiesced.

It hasn't been tried yet, but you have to wonder what kind of response Realm or Corn would get if they organized some of their fellow College Republicans and started yelling at a guest speaker like Senator Bernie Sanders. (We asked them, and as you might imagine, they aren't keen on trying. They don't think it would end well, and it's hard to argue with that conclusion.) Interestingly, like Ted Kennedy before him (1983), Bernie Sanders actually *did* speak at Liberty University (the Christian college founded by the late "intolerant" Reverend Jerry Falwell) in 2015. As the *New York Times* reported, "Mr. Sanders, who is Jewish, was greeted politely by the crowd."[1]

When conservative speakers get shouted down, at least they get to leave campus. But the students who organize and host the events have to stay in the cesspool of intolerance.

When Kassy Dillon brought up the idea of hosting Ben Shapiro at Mount Holyoke College, the Student Government Association held an "emergency meeting" on free speech. Dillon found out about it from a professor (no, the meeting organizers didn't think to invite her) and showed up. From her spot in the audience, she watched leftist professors discuss whether "hate speech" counted as free speech. During the question and answer section, a student called her out by name.

"We wouldn't even be having this discussion," she recalls him saying, "if it wasn't for Kassy Dillon inviting bigots to our campus."

Universities' allowing the forces of political correctness to disrupt and disturb the free flow of ideas is bad enough. But for some students, it gets much worse.

Dillon got a dose of this reality after a 2016 election night party.

In the spirit of coming together after a bitter campaign, Dillon's College Republican group accepted an invitation to co-sponsor an election results watch party at Mount Holyoke's campus center. Like just about everyone else, they expected Hillary Clinton to win. But as the night wore on, and it became clearer that Donald Trump would prevail, the spirit of amicable bipartisanship faded.

Dillon said angry partygoers shouted at her and pedestrians jumped in front of her car as she drove home. A good night's sleep did nothing to quell their anger; as she walked to class the next day, a fellow student put her arm around Dillon and asked with mock friendliness, "How's it going, bigot?"

And as bad as the childish temper tantrums and name calling can get, some of the harassment conservative students face can be downright scary.

⊘

Morgan Realm was lucky—her face was not very recognizable on the flyer targeting her. Some of her fellow College Republican board members weren't as lucky.

Just after the Tommy Robinson debacle, Realm and her fellow board members found their faces and personal information on flyers hung around campus like wanted posters. The New York City chapter of Antifa hand-posted the flyers, urging people to "let [the college Republicans] know what you think."

The practice is known as "doxing"—giving out contact information with the intent to initiate harassment.

On the other side of the country, at the birthplace of the Free Speech movement, Pranav Jandhyala has dealt with the same thing.

Jandhyala—the University of California-Berkeley student who suffered a concussion during the February 2017 campus riot—has found pictures of himself on local Antifa organizing websites. But even when he catches them in the act, he told us, Berkeley's administration refuses to intervene.

"I film it, and I photograph it," Jandhyala told Dennis of the doxing. "And whenever I present it to the University, they never take action."

The personal targeting of Jandhyala is the latest in a list of harassment of College Republicans at Berkeley by campus leftists. It runs the gamut from physical violence to tearing down signs to destruction of materials. Despite repeated pleas, the university refuses to step in. Jandhyala can't help but wonder: if his group held views that aligned more with the administrators, would the harassment still be handled with such a cavalier attitude?

"These administrators sympathize with these students [who commit the attacks]," he said. "And sometimes they even feel it's justified to attack us."

⊘

When we decided to use the title *No Safe Spaces* for our campus tour, our movie, and this book, we thought we were being clever. But for some students, it's eerily accurate.

Administrators, faculty, and others on the left talk about safe spaces, but only for the right people. Or, more accurately, the left people. For people on the right, there really are no safe spaces at many colleges and universities.

This is unfair to people on the right. But how condescending is it to people on the left? How insulting to their intelligence to think they can't handle opposing views? And it's especially demented to believe that those opposing views are so dangerous that they have to be shut down with aggression or even violence.

⊘

For some of Cornell University's conservative "Marranos," Olivia Corn offered a one-person "safe space."

"When I was president of [the] Cornell Republicans," she told Dennis, "I used to get messages all the time from people who would say, 'Hey, just want to let you know I'm a Republican, but I don't feel comfortable saying it.'" Those messages would thank her for speaking up for the students who chose not to. Every now and then, one of her correspondents would ask if they could get together for coffee. Some students just wanted to connect with someone who had a similar philosophy.

Corn estimates she received close to a hundred messages from students who worried that if anyone else knew what they thought, they would suffer lost friendships or falling grades.

"I understand where they're coming from," said Corn. "That was something that I struggled with, too." Even as a freshman, she understood the risks of being politically active on campus and weighed them heavily before "outing" herself as a conservative by joining the College Republicans.

In the years since, she has lost friends and suffered through biased classes. At one point, while she was walking back to her dorm after a meeting, an assailant swore at her, called her a racist, and pushed her down a hill. (Corn was more stunned than hurt; the assailant was never identified or prosecuted.)

Still, Corn has no regrets about being outspoken. She welcomes the adversity that her left-leaning counterparts cower from.

"I've told people that this is what I believe. Deal with it."

CHAPTER EIGHT

WHERE ARE THE ADULTS?

I n July 2017, Adam had a chance to tell the United States Congress some of the things we've been telling college audiences for a while. Flanked by the likes of Ben Shapiro, who has been threatened, protested, and booted from campus, and Nadine Strossen, former ACLU President and founder of Feminists for Free Expression, Adam was invited to a joint subcommittee hearing to discuss "Challenges to Freedom of Speech on College Campuses." Mark and director Justin Folk accompanied Adam to the hearing and Mark noticed the contrast between Ben's and Adam's preparations. Whereas Ben had neatly typed single-spaced testimony, Adam sat in the green room, grabbed a yellow legal pad and a pen, and began to sketch out his thoughts.

The witnesses sat, pens and notepads laid before them, waiting patiently to give testimony.

When the committee reached Adam, he held his notepad, looked at the committee members, and asked the question that no one else had dared ask: "Do we get to keep these pads?"

"And not that I'm going to, but what do you reckon they'll get on eBay?"

Hearings can be boring, and this was a welcome moment of levity. But Adam's original plan called for something much more drastic. You see, Adam really wanted to show up before Congress in his pajamas. It was a gimmick, yes—but one with a serious message. Adam wanted to say, "Let's put censorship to bed." Not everyone thought this was a prudent idea. As Adam's producer, Mark was literally on the phone negotiating with congressional staff, who were begging him, "Pease don't do this! We're taking a huge risk. We can't tell you not to wear pajamas, but please don't."

He didn't (in fact, he wore a suit and necktie).

Joking aside, Adam was honored to have a chance to talk to Congress about this challenging issue. Obviously, we think it's pretty important, or we wouldn't be touring college campuses, and we wouldn't have made a movie about it. Yet the need for a Congressional hearing illustrates a disturbing fact: not only do colleges and universities have a mission-threatening problem with free speech and free expression, but they are surrendering their responsibility to handle the problem. They are letting responsibility move up the chain and passing the proverbial buck.

Given his childhood, Adam can offer an informed opinion about deadbeat dads and checked-out moms abdicating responsibility. His mother, a free-range hippie, leaned on the government and family members for assistance. Adam's childhood home had been gifted by his maternal grandparents, and he watched it suffer from lack of attention. That's not something that happens in a house that you own after saving up for a down payment and getting your credit shored up for a mortgage. It's certainly not something that happens if your landlord could kick you out at any time. But since her father had bought the house and handed it over to her, Adam's mom felt no moral obligation to worry about its upkeep.

A parent gave his daughter an easy way out, and the daughter got lazy and felt entitled. (We will see that pattern again, so if you're taking notes, write that down.)

Despite the gift of housing, Adam's mom still leaned on welfare, food stamps, and whatever other government program for which she qualified to avoid work. Young Adam once asked if she would get a job; she replied that if she did, she risked losing her welfare benefits. This wasn't a case of using government help to create a nurturing, fulfilling homelife as a stay-at-home mother, either. She wasn't helping Adam and his sister do their homework each night or doling out discipline if they stepped out of line. She did teach moral relativism, telling Adam that there was no right or wrong in the Cold War between the United States and the communist Soviet Union. She also took every opportunity to remind her kids how brutal white people had been to non-whites. After the family watched the miniseries *Roots*, Alex Haley's largely fictional story of his family's history as African-American slaves, she said, "Look how horrible we are." It didn't make sense to young

Adam—his family couldn't figure out how to buy a house. Why should they get blamed because some other people more than a hundred years before had thought it was okay to buy and sell people? (Besides, his father's family had still been in Italy when all that was happening.)

There are a few times in this book, during the *No Safe Spaces* film, and during our tour, when we describe college students as "kids." That word gets used a lot to describe people on the sunny, less-back-achy, all-your-joints-are-still-spongy-and-working side of thirty; but for college students, the word works.

When people enter college, they're usually around eighteen years old. They're no closer, time-wise, to entering the workforce as adults than they are to the point when they started high school. Just a two-term presidency ago, they were ten years old. Now, if you're twenty-one and storming the beaches of Normandy, I'll lay off the paternalistic talk. But if you're toiling away at Hagerstown Junior College, the label probably applies.

Kids don't have perspective. They have an inflated sense of their own life experience, which makes sense given that they don't have all that much of it yet. When they head to college and get that first year under their belt, kids feel like they have everything figured out by the second year. (Did you know that the word "sophomore" comes from the Greek language and literally translates to "wise fool"? It's true. The "more" part has the same root as the word "moron.")

Undergraduate education doesn't exactly promote adulthood. By their junior and senior years, some students may have moved off campus; but they typically aren't working nine-to-five jobs and finishing their degrees at night. (If you are in that category, good for you.)

Once upon a time, we had rites of passage. A young man might have to kill a lion to prove he was capable of protecting his family and to be a member of his tribe in good standing. Today, turning eighteen qualifies you to cancel out Dennis Prager's vote.

These students may be legal adults, but really they are children when they head off to school, and even for some time after that. College may offer them more freedom, but for the majority of those matriculating, it's really an extension of childhood.

And what a childhood they can boast about!

We live in a time when children grow up dipped in Purell, playing soccer games where no one keeps score, and watching dreck like *Wow! Wow! Wubbzy!* (Have you seen some of today's children's programming? In the old days, kids would watch cartoons where good guys fought bad guys, or where heroes went on adventures. Think *G.I. Joe*, *Scooby Doo*, *Land of the Lost*, or even *The Smurfs*. Today, we sit toddlers down in front of stupid shows with bright colors, mindless songs, and vague lessons about friendship or table manners.)

The old practice of sending children to go play outside and telling them to come back when the streetlights came on taught them autonomy. It left them to their own devices and let them forge their own friendships. In contrast, modern helicopter parents overschedule and over-supervise play dates. Pickup games of sandlot baseball and playground basketball have given way to regimented, feel-good sports leagues where everyone gets a trophy and no one loses, lest anyone have to suffer hurt feelings. (Kudos for showing up to the field, kids! Way to go, existing! Congrats on having a mom with a minivan!)

Children suffer from too much protection and micro-management of their lives—but also from the absence of authority. As much as we make fun of Hillary Clinton's book, *It Takes a Village*, there was a time when parents could rely on a network of adults—teachers, principals, friends, and neighbors—to reinforce what the child was being taught at home. If an old Jewish lady caught a young Dennis misbehaving on the subway, by the time he got home to Max and Hilda, he was in for a tongue lashing (or worse). Aside from being jerks who enjoyed yelling at kids and narking on them, that network of adults actually served a civilizing purpose. By reining in bad behavior, they helped guarantee the rights that we as a society had generally agreed on as part of the social contract. They enforced rules of mutual respect.

No longer. That network is gone with the wind. You've heard of helicopter parents who hover over their children, eager to rescue them from the slightest misfortune, haven't you? That's nothing compared to another recent trend: bulldozer parents. Bulldozer parents clear the way for their children, pushing aside any obstruction. When their precious little snowflake angel gets a D in algebra, these parents rush to the school and demand to know why. They blame the teacher instead of encouraging their own child to study harder and get better at math. These are the parents who bark at umpires at Little League games. Delightful.

Kids pick up on subtle messages more than we realize, including the lessons that parents teach with this kind of behavior. By the time they graduate high school, they have had it drilled into their mushy little heads that they are perfect creatures: the pinnacle of the universe's machinations. And as if we hadn't messed them up enough already, by middle school and high school most kids have their own smartphones. This small, innocent-looking piece of equipment is actually the gateway to a polarizing, depressing, and self-aggrandizing addiction: social media.

After eighteen years of this, kids head off to colleges and universities that have abandoned their original mission of rigorous academic inquiry in favor of politically correct culture.

Remember that the impetus behind political correctness, speech codes, trigger warnings, and safe spaces was the same impetus behind all these parenting trends: protection. And you can see how the system perpetuates itself. Politically correct colleges protect students. Those students graduate and coddle their own children in cotton wool. Those children go to college with the expectation that they'll be handled with kid gloves, so schools become even more politically correct. The cycle continues, getting worse with each generation.

Administrators recognized the growing diversity on campuses (starting in the 1950s and exploding in the 1960s and 1970s), and they foresaw the potential for tensions, with so many diverse cultures coming together. Restrictions on overtly racist speech evolved into restrictions on any speech that could be considered racist. Diversity and representation trumped education. Now students are taught that the game is rigged—either privileged majorities or an evil patriarchy is conspiring against them.

Schools erase Shakespeare from their English curricula and America's Founding Fathers from their history classes for the same reason youth sports leagues stop keeping soccer scores: they don't want anyone feeling hurt or left out. And in both cases, handling the children with such over-the-top care and attention creates an unearned sense of entitlement. If you try to prevent students from dealing with difficulty, soon they begin to expect (nay, demand) that level of comfort.

Have you ever been upgraded to first class for just one leg of a flight? You are miraculously bumped up (with free drinks) for the first flight; then you have a layover somewhere, after which you try to cram yourself back into coach for the second half of the flight. Once you get used to the legroom in first class, suddenly coach feels like it's a couple of degrees removed from a cattle car.

Now imagine being an eighteen-year-old kid who grew up being catered to by her parents. Then on day one of college, she is told that no one should be made to feel uncomfortable by an idea. Given the constant reinforcement of these "special snowflake" messages, how is she going to react when someone offers an insight or a concept that doesn't quite fit her worldview, the same worldview she hears in the classroom every day?

Remember what Greg Lukianoff said. When FIRE started out, they often worked with students to fight speech codes. Now they see students pushing for the speech codes. It's because students feel entitled to limit what others are saying. They have been protected from any kind of uncomfortable experience for decades.

Even for those kids who start out with conservative beliefs, if they don't have a strong handle on their views and values, relentless propaganda from professors, administrators, campus leaders, and peers makes it very difficult to hold onto them.

Because they are emotionally immature at that age, students can get swept away by the ideas that surround them in their new environment. And they naturally want to see themselves as morally virtuous;

once you insist on your own virtue, it's a short jump to deeming those you disagree with morally repugnant. Once you've made that jump, silencing their speech doesn't seem so bad. In fact, it's the logical conclusion. Who doesn't want to tell the devil to shut his yap?

It is hard to blame them, any more than you would blame a toddler for creating a crayon mural on the living room wall. They are doing what comes naturally, under the circumstances. But that doesn't mean we should incentivize more of the same behavior.

Let's say you come around the corner into your living room and find your three-year-old daughter beaming next to purple scribbles marring the wall next to the sofa. If you pat her on the head, coo over her creativity, and tell her how beautiful her artwork is, what do you think is going to happen next? An orange installation in the kitchen will soon follow. Perhaps next she'll move from crayons to watercolors or markers. She will think you approve; therefore, she will try to keep pleasing you with more and more artwork.

On the other hand, if you yell at her and tell her never to do it again, she'll get the message. You could make her help clean off the wall, too.

It is difficult to hear challenging viewpoints—that is why they're "challenging" in the first place. A person's first visceral reaction is to shy away from views he doesn't like. His second, even more primal, reaction is to want those views shut down. As in the case of the toddler artist crafting a Crayola-on-drywall masterpiece, though, it's up to the adult in the room to correct the bad behavior.

But instead of correcting bad behavior, school administrators have compounded the original sin of political correctness by giving the loudest students *carte blanche* to wield a speech-silencing cudgel.

When conservative groups bring speakers to campus or a center-right voice is tapped for a commencement address, leftist students protest and demand the speaking invitation be rescinded, with at least the tacit consent of faculty and administration.

The desire to shut down conversation is not the move of people who are confident in their beliefs. People who are comfortable in their sexuality don't need to boast about their conquests. Confident people can listen to other points of view. Mark's kids watch CNN, MSNBC, and Fox News. He's not afraid that they might hear the other tribe's political propaganda and be instantly seduced by it. Of course, the possibility that some student might actually be persuaded by exposure to a speech made on campus is never cited as a reason for shutting down a lecture.

When students want to invite someone like Ben Shapiro to the University of California Berkeley or some other campus with an active political Left, the administration blocks the visit because they worry about mob violence. Instead of outright banning speakers, another tactic is to charge extra under the guise of what's called a "high-profile speaker policy." For example, they might charge conservatives three times more for Ben Shapiro than they would charge a leftist group that wanted to bring Supreme Court Justice Sonia Sotomayor to campus. In December of 2018, conservative groups reached settlement with U.C. Berkeley prohibiting the school from tacking on security fees based on concerns that the "viewpoints, opinions, or anticipated expression" of guest speakers "might provoke disturbances."

This is a positive development. If there's a violent mob on campus, it isn't Ben Shapiro's fault—he's just someone coming to campus to talk about ideas. Mob violence is the mob's fault. It's the people throwing Molotov cocktails, chucking rocks at cops, or threatening the students who invited Shapiro in the first place who should be held responsible.

As for those students who are trying to silence conservative speakers whose opinions they don't agree with, the administration should be telling them, in no uncertain terms, that they are wrong.

It is completely fine to disagree with someone. It's completely appropriate to ask challenging questions of a guest speaker. And it's absolutely appropriate to counter offensive speech with more speech, written or spoken. But it is not okay to restrict someone else's speech because you disagree with him.

That is what we need school administrators to say right now. And they aren't doing it.

⊘

We've talked about some of the reasons professors have for letting academics—the reason for the academy, by the way—go off the rails. But why do administrators sit by and let the inmates run the asylum?

Politically speaking, the oppression typically goes one way. You don't see Noam Chomsky getting chased out of a guest lecture by an angry mob. No college is going to let "scope and logistics" prevent Barack Obama from gracing their campus. When free speech gets clipped, it's usually people from the center-right getting hushed.

The administrators don't agree with that type of speech in the first place, so they are more likely to go along with their kindred spirits in shutting it down. They're not usually really malicious, and it's not some kind of conspiracy. It's just that the administrators have the same blind spot as their students: when they hear something with which they disagree, they don't feel the need to stick their necks out to make sure it is heard.

Parents who raise precious snowflakes and administrators who coddle them make the situation in higher education nearly impossible to fix. If just one side was the bad influence, you might hope the other side could balance the equation. But the combination of modern hyper-parenting and left-leaning professors and administrators has allowed students to remake universities into large-scale editions of the island in *Lord of the Flies*.

Solutions will not emerge on their own. They will require personal responsibility on the part of people raising kids and people teaching kids.

You get a lot of flak on campus nowadays if you say you want boys to man up and become men. Some people suggest it's sexist. They never have a problem with girls becoming women, though. The phrase means to grow up. Whatever gender you are or identify as, at some point you have to become an adult.

All of us who are adults right now have to step up and act like adults. It is up to us to say, "This is nonsense." It's up to parents to raise tougher, more independent children who can go to college and choose not to be offended by every person who expresses an opinion with which they disagree. It's up to faculty and administrators to have the resolve to say, "So what?" when students complain about being offended—and tell them to suck it up and deal with it.

It is up to all of us to realize that we know more about the world than an eighteen-year-old kid does (even if the eighteen-year-old kid doesn't understand that), and it's our job to help that kid learn more. It is our job to guide them and help them mold their brains into functioning adult minds that can think and reason and enjoy life.

Like Whitney Houston, we believe the children are the future. But adults are in charge in the present, and we should start acting like it.

CHAPTER NINE

LOSING THE AMERICAN TRINITY

R ace and ethnicity define nearly every nation on Earth.

With one major exception: the United States of America.

If you want to be English, you have to be born of English stock—or at least in England. If you're from an ethnic minority, even being born in China isn't good enough to make you Chinese in the eyes of China's majority population. But Americans come from every race and ethnicity in the world, and we can be born anywhere—because our country is based on ideas.

And it works! America is the greatest country ever invented.

What are the ideas on which America is based? Years ago Dennis
Prager named these ideas "The American Trinity"—based on the
three mottos that appear on American money:

- *E Pluribus Unum*
- Liberty
- In God We Trust

The first motto, the Latin phrase *E Pluribus Unum,* is literally
translated, "Out of Many, One." If you know your Revolutionary
War history, it's easy to see where this idea originally came from. The
thirteen American colonies united to defeat the British and win their
independence. Then they went on to form the United States.

The trials and tribulations of the American forces during the
Revolutionary War included going up against what was at the time
the greatest military force in the world. After the war, when it came
time to decide how to govern the new nation, cooperation between
states was crucial. The Constitutional Convention in Philadelphia
pitted large states against small states, states with major urban centers
against agrarian states, and, yes, free states against states with econ-
omies based on slavery. To create our Constitution, our founding
fathers had to balance all of those competing interests. Even though
they had to hash out some of the differences in an extremely violent
conflict four score and seven years later, that Constitution has given
us the framework on which we built our great nation.

As America has grown, the meaning of *E Pluribus Unum* has
evolved. Waves of immigrants have come to America, adding in their

own cultural elements as they assimilate to the broader American society.

This is unique to the United States. People can move to other nations, but they can't join the society like new Americans can. Turkish people have emigrated throughout Western Europe over the past several years, but a Turk who moves to Sweden will never be a Swede. If you come to America, however, you can become a citizen, have the same rights as everyone else, and be considered a true American by your fellow citizens. You also might have jury duty. That's a small price to pay, but it's there.

We should revel in the unity of our country—built out of a multiplicity of cultures and ethnicities. But our colleges and universities are more interested in finding the cracks and divisions in America than they are in celebrating our common ground.

⊘

America's second motto is "Liberty."

As we've seen, the idea that all humans yearn to be free is a romantic notion. In reality, the greater yearning of the human species is to be cared for, not to be free.

Freedom and liberty must be taught and internalized. And these teachings also run contrary to another common value—equality.

It makes sense that many schools teach the American Revolution and the French Revolution at the same time. After all, they happened around the same time, and the former was obviously an inspiration for the latter. But comparing the three-part French

Revolution motto—"Liberty, Equality, Fraternity"—with ours reveals big differences.

As it turns out, parts one and two of the French slogan are in direct conflict with each other.

Before the French Revolution, some people—the aristocracy and the clergy—had reached greater heights within society. The revolutionaries famously used the guillotine to cut them down to size and correct that perceived problem.

We Americans do believe in equality—but our idea of equality is equality before the law. We all expect to be treated the same as everyone else when it comes to our interactions with government—by judges and juries, representatives, and government bureaucrats. If a poor person calls the fire department, he should get the same fire truck that his rich neighbor would get if his house were on fire. A black person who is arrested should enjoy the same presumption of innocence as a white person. Even if that doesn't always happen, that's our expectation.

The type of equality enforced by the guillotine in the French Revolution—which, unfortunately, is also the kind of equality that most people, even in America, talk about today—is equality of outcomes. But you cannot have equality of outcomes and still have freedom.

In America, or any truly free society, your success or failure is based on your own effort, intelligence, and luck—which are different from everyone else's.

On college campuses, the tension between liberty and equality fuels much of the discussion surrounding protected classes, victimhood mentality, and identity politics. You certainly see the impulse for equality in accusations of "white privilege." You also see the drive to enforce equality in the notion of "safe spaces"—which protect one group of people by limiting what others are allowed to say.

$$\oslash$$

The third and final of America's trinity of mottos is "In God We Trust."

This isn't a clarion call for everyone to run out to church on Sunday. In fact, America is rare among nations in that it has no state religion—in fact our Constitution specifically forbids the government from establishing one. What "In God We Trust" means is that America is based on Judeo-Christian values, which manifest themselves in our understanding of our God-given rights. The Declaration of Independence says that all people "are endowed by their Creator with certain unalienable Rights, that among these are Life, Liberty and the pursuit of Happiness."

In other words, we are born with our rights. Government doesn't give us the right to say what we like, to worship (or not worship) as we think we should, or to work to better ourselves and our family. The only time we wouldn't have those rights is if exercising them would interfere unfairly with someone else's rights. Government only exists to make sure that no one interferes with our rights and that we don't interfere with anyone else's.

"In God We Trust" also defines our expectations for each other as citizens. Human beings are not inherently good. We can behave well, or we can behave badly. "In God We Trust" acknowledges a higher authority as our reason for good behavior. It makes us take responsibility for our own actions and holds us accountable. Maybe, like Dennis, you believe in the God of the Bible, who exists in heaven and judges you when you hurt other people. Maybe, like Adam, you're an atheist, and you don't think people should act like jerks. Maybe you're somewhere in between. It doesn't matter—it's not the government's responsibility to set your moral compass.

The alternative is a government that doesn't just protect your rights, but also tells you how to live your life. If you're kind to other people because it's part of your moral code, you're a good person. If you're kind to others because you're worried about being punished if you aren't, then you're just someone trying to avoid getting a $50 "you're being a jerk" ticket from your local law enforcement.

Compare that with the politically correct restrictions on campus speech. If you assume everyone who is speaking their mind is doing so as part of an earnest attempt to educate himself or herself, then any perceived slight against you—from an insensitive phrase to a flawed assumption about life experience—can be considered accidental. If you assume goodwill and you're legitimately offended by something, it's fairly easy to write off the offense as accidental. You can expect that if you calmly correct the "microaggression" you'd find it wasn't at all intended as aggressive.

If, on the other hand, you support things like speech codes, you're taking away the responsibility from the people speaking. If people are told what to say and how to say it, they can't be polite. Politeness involves choice, and you have stripped away that choice.

⊘

As a country, we obviously haven't lived up perfectly to our ideals. But that doesn't change the fact that these are the ideals to which

Americans aspire. They give us a road map, or a societal GPS, so that when we do fall short (because we aren't perfect), we can get back on track.

And can we talk about just how far we've gotten with those ideals? When people say, "We've come so far, but we still have so far to go," it's a little infuriating. When our country started out, voting was limited to white landowning men. They didn't even just want to limit it to white men; they threw in that landowning thing to make voting super exclusive. It took some time to change it, but now all citizens eighteen and over can vote (unless they've done something to forfeit that right). We elected a black president. We almost elected a woman president. Women and minorities as governors, senators, and even Oscar hosts isn't groundbreaking anymore. It is actually significant that we aren't more excited by these achievements, as they've become part of our normal culture.

Government didn't initiate these advances, either. They didn't come from someone sitting in an official office somewhere, thinking up ways to give up power. They reflect advances in a society and an electorate that decides who sits in that office. Great social movements in America—civil rights, expanding suffrage, and so forth—tend to start with the people and end with the government being dragged into changing, rather than the other way around.

Capitalism is America's economic system because of the way it fits those ideals. For long-term success in a capitalist economy, you have to be open to new opportunities, and you have to operate honestly. You will only get as far as your brain and your work ethic take you.

On campus, all you'll hear about is our failure to perfectly meet our ideals: Slavery is the sin America will never pay down. Our society is misogynistic and hostile toward women. Our immigration system punishes Hispanic and Latino families. Gays and lesbians live under a cloud of hatred.

Don't even get them started on capitalism.

And then they get so obsessed with America's shortcomings, they go completely off the rails.

You'll hear professors praising Cuba. They'll throw out statistics that paint the Communist prison state as a little island paradise where no one wants for anything. It's hard to listen to. They love using statistics from Cuba's government. (How solid are those numbers? You can trust Cuban government figures the way you can trust a space shuttle made of tin cans and a cherry bomb.) Not to mention that Cuban prisons are full of people who would love to discuss quality of life. Or maybe they wouldn't, since speaking their mind got them locked up in the first place.

You hear these professors praising dictators, and it makes you wonder how they can believe what they're saying. Their eagerness to point out America's flaws makes them ready to jump into rhetorical bed with any Tom, Dick, or Fidel wearing fatigues and yelling "Death to America!"

Colleges and universities' reflexive opposition to the most fundamental American values has two very poisonous effects. One is sad, and the other is downright dangerous.

The first consequence is that colleges will churn out graduates who can't function in American society. If you spend your formative years hearing that nothing that happens to you is your responsibility, how will you succeed in a world where that isn't the reality?

A certain few will head back to campus and enroll in a master's program in interdisciplinary post-modern comic book studies. So they're taken care of. What about the rest? Even if they're hired and manage to hold down a job, will they understand what it takes to excel in their chosen field? At best they'll just survive—and that will be it. Survival. Getting by.

Think of all the lost potential for success.

The direr consequence of forgetting American values is that students will graduate and expect society to bend to them. Unfortunately, society is gradually starting to comply.

If we trade in the American trinity—*E Pluribus Unum*, Liberty, and In God We Trust—for the values currently being taught on college campuses, we risk losing the ideals that make America America. We will be trading in a value system that empowers people to direct their own fate for one that promotes equality over freedom. We will exchange a society that tries to correct (but never forget) its sins for one that lets old wounds fester. We will abandon a system proven to give people a chance to elevate themselves from oppression and poverty for one that wallows in suffering as an excuse for failure.

As graduates leave campus, they shape their workplaces and neighborhoods. They get married and raise families. They change the world around them in both big and small ways. Those who shaped them in their college years (when they were coming of age intellectually and philosophically) will inform those changes.

Through their graduates, colleges become the leading edge of society.

And tomorrow's graduates—who are today's college students—don't cherish the American trinity like previous generations. Over time, a poorly educated populace is forgetting the original ideas of America's Founding Fathers. Companies eager to hire the best talent must create "safe spaces" in the workplace. Entertainers must include "trigger warnings" in case their material might offend someone. Voters look more and more to an ever-expanding government not to protect their rights, but instead to preserve their comfort at the expense of their freedoms.

The fight for free speech at colleges and universities is a proxy fight for these American values, and the battle does not stop at the campus gates.

Sorry if it sounds like we're going a tad over the top with this. Obviously, we love this country and want to see everyone have a chance at the kind of success we have. We don't want to see a wave of college graduates unwittingly reverse almost 250 years of progress and turn the American experiment into a failure.

We feel a sense of urgency in conveying this message because, if you look closely, you'll see it's already happening.

CHAPTER TEN

POLITICAL CORRECTNESS MOVES OFF-CAMPUS

YouTube, owned by Google, isn't just the world's biggest video-sharing platform.

Since its launch in 2005, YouTube has revolutionized the way people communicate online. Combined with video-capable smartphones and ever cheaper and user-friendlier editing software, now anyone can be a video star. If you're an independent filmmaker, a wannabe talk show host, or an aspiring cartoonist, you have an easy way to get your creations in front of a worldwide audience.

YouTube is the place to make it happen...if they'll let you.

In 2011, Dennis started Prager University, or PragerU, to help fill in where colleges and universities have failed. Through concise five-minute videos, PragerU instructors—including four former prime ministers, three Pulitzer Prize winners, professors, Adam(!), and even some liberals—apply solid research and logic to a wide range of issues facing America. You can check out videos about international affairs, economics, culture, society, and science, all free of charge and featuring learned subject matter experts.

In seven years, the project has been a rousing success. By 2019, PragerU videos had reached a total of 1.7 billion views on YouTube. Seven out of ten viewers have reported changing their minds on an important issue after watching a PragerU video, with 86 percent referencing the videos during online discussions. The videos are meant to reach younger people, and they're doing it: 65 percent of PragerU video viewers are under the age of thirty-five.

(The PragerU football team is still winless, but you can't do everything at once, right?)

That success comes despite YouTube arbitrarily deciding to censor nearly one hundred PragerU videos by putting them in "restricted mode," which relegated them to the same category as videos with adult content and violence. If you tried to access one of these PragerU videos at a school or on a shared family computer with restricted mode enabled to protect kids from stumbling across something they shouldn't see, no dice.

And what sketchy content was Dennis peddling that triggered this response? The restricted videos include an explanation of America's involvement in the Korean War, a discussion of racism in law enforcement, and an explanation of Israel's founding. Some of the topics are controversial, but the videos themselves include no objectionable content. They simply argue a side.

Adam was the instructor on one of those videos. His lecture was titled, "Who NOT to Vote For," and he managed to make his point while keeping his language squarely on the PG level. His thesis: "Don't trust politicians who promise to take care of you." How is that even a controversial stance? People have been complaining about broken campaign promises for as long as democracy has existed. (No doubt there are cave drawings in France somewhere critical of Governor Thag for his failure to put a mammoth carcass in every pot.) But in YouTube's view, kids shouldn't see a video telling them that the person promising them free stuff isn't legit. Isn't anyone worried about conflicting messages we send to kids? "Hey, don't trust the guy promising you free candy from the back of a windowless white van. Instead, trust the guy promising free candy from the bed of a rented pickup truck with bales of hay strategically placed around him."

YouTube has not offered specifics about what makes these particular PragerU videos so naughty that you can only view them behind the virtual black curtain. They refer back to their terms of service—the arbitrary, self-written, and ever-changing rules that dictate what users can do on and with their platform. As on many other social media platforms, those terms offer YouTube great latitude and legal cover to do just about anything they want, and they can be changed at the company's discretion.

Anna Jane Parrill, a program manager at the Foundation for Economic Education, has seen a change in how YouTube operates over the years, with the site administrators becoming "more of the morality police than they used to be."

As Parrill observed, "Originally it was designed to have anyone host whatever video they wanted, and that was kind of cool." At that time YouTube "was the great equalizer.... an amazing place to share ideas—anyone's ideas."

Then, Parrill explained, YouTube found ways to downgrade videos without completely banning them. For example, the social media platform would "demonetize" videos – banning advertising on certain videos, and cutting off a stream of revenue to some creators while allowing it for others.

In PragerU's case, YouTube has judged the ideas discussed in these videos as potentially offensive or dangerous, so they put up barriers to make the videos harder to find and limit audience exposure.

Sounds familiar, doesn't it?

$\oslash$

One of the knocks on the politically correct environment on campus is that by trying to shield students from challenging thoughts or ideas, colleges and universities are failing to prepare students to function in the real world, where challenging thoughts and ideas will come at them all the time.

FIRE's CEO Greg Lukianoff, whom we first met back in chapter two, says he sees a more disturbing trend.

As schools flood the work force with graduates who were educated in an environment of so-called "safe spaces," the "real world" is bending to accommodate the expectations of these recent grads.

"Once we create an expectation that it's a nice thing to do censor people and in an 'enlightened' way," warns Lukianoff, "there's no reason to believe that they're not going construct a world that looks like that."

He's right.

Scroll through the business headlines, and you won't go far before you find spokespeople for large companies dropping buzzwords like "social responsibility" and "corporate citizenship." It's virtue signaling: they're trying to position their company as a champion of the environment, equality, and the historically oppressed.

Remember when the Supreme Court's 2015 decision in *Obergefell v. Hodges* legalized same-sex marriages in all fifty states? Companies couldn't get on Twitter fast enough to celebrate. AT&T, Target, Visa, Maytag, Uber, Lyft, Jell-O, MTV, Whole Foods, Tide, Ben & Jerry's, and hundreds more companies tweeted out rainbow-colored products or versions of their corporate logo with the hashtag #LoveWins.

Even Honey Maid, most famous for their graham crackers, tweeted in support of the ruling. Congratulations to those of you who viewed the *Obergefell* case as the momentous summit of a decades-long climb to equality. You may have had to face intolerance and isolation from your own friends and family, but surely it warms your heart to know that Honey Maid graham crackers approves of your love. (Interestingly, Sylvester Graham was a Presbyterian minister who believed his crackers could help people abstain from sexual activity—but that's another story.)

Can you imagine anyone caring what a graham cracker company has to say about social issues? Yet Honey Maid had to let everyone know that they care.

They didn't care enough for some. The same weekend the verdict was released, Mic's senior editor, Darnell Moore (who is black and gay), complained that the celebration over the *Obergefell* ruling threatened to overshadow the Black Lives Matter movement. A week later, Alysha Light, founder of California-based FlightPR, wrote in

Digiday, "Why aren't brands as willing to support #BlackLivesMatter in the same way they were with #LoveWins?"

(Ben & Jerry's did release a Black Lives Matter-branded ice cream flavor, so we're clearly on the way to racial harmony now.)

Celebrities get the same treatment. In November 2017 the *Guardian* published an unsigned editorial wondering when pop star Taylor Swift would speak out against Trump.[1] Everyone else of consequence had made their feelings known, the piece reasoned, so what was Swift waiting for? (The shaming finally paid off. After years of pressure, Swift capitulated in 2018, endorsing Democrats Phil Bredesen for U.S. Senate and Jim Cooper for House of Representatives.)[2]

It isn't enough to care about one leftist cause. Every public entity—whether a musician, an actor, or a corporation—has to care about all of them.

It may seem like social justice warriors will stop at nothing until everyone aligns their brand with the Left's values. But standing up against the pressure can work: just ask Hobby Lobby owners David and Barbara Green, who had their own brush with the Supreme Court in 2014.

The Greens are Christians, so they have deep religious convictions against abortifacient birth control methods. As a result, they decided those methods would not be covered in the health benefit plans they offered their employees. When the federal government tried to force the Greens to cover those birth control methods, they refused. When the Supreme Court ruled in favor of Hobby Lobby, protestors outside the Supreme Court building waved signs that read, "My Birth Control, My Decision." They should have read, "My Birth Control. My Decision. You Pay for It."

How dare Hobby Lobby impose their personal views on their employees or the public? (Unless they're draping their corporate logo in rainbow colors.)

The difference between Hobby Lobby and the companies that make a big deal of their supposed "corporate values" in support of same sex marriage is that the latter are caving to pressure from the most vocal members of society, and the former is not. Companies who change their social media avatars to rainbow flags aren't being brave; they're following the crowd.

While these companies may honestly support these politically correct positions, let's be realistic. They wouldn't say anything if they thought talking a stand would result in lost revenue. Instead, they tie their brand identities to social causes because they know the consumers entering the workforce are clutching a diploma from an institution that just spent four years telling them that taking popular social stances is important and that stepping outside the realm of orthodox thought is not. They have been taught to care whether their graham crackers think it's okay for gay people to get married.

Politics don't really matter to most of these companies; they're just trying to avoid bad publicity and boycotts. Social justice is hardly essential to their brand. Honey Maid could start putting Che Guevara on its box and calling its product "Commie Crackers"; but if you're enjoying a campfire s'more, you aren't going to turn to your fellow campers and say, "You know, these are sweet but not as sweet as throwing off the yoke of imperialism."

Unfortunately, some of the companies susceptible to this political pressure are companies that define how we see the world.

Technology companies like Facebook, Google, Instagram, Twitter, and others have to cater to new graduates as few others do. They need to stay on the cutting edge, and they constantly need new workers who understand the latest trends and technology. On top of that, their industry is expanding. They have jobs to fill, and they need people. These companies are a natural landing spot for recent graduates, which also makes them an extension of the campus values those grads bring with them.

James Damore worried about close-mindedness on campus—not a college campus, but the Google corporate campus in Palo Alto, California. He also worried about efforts to close the so-called "gender gap" in the tech industry (information technology remains a largely male-dominated field).

In 2017, Damore wrote a memo entitled, "Google's Ideological Echo Chamber," in which he explored some of the reasons why women were not well represented in tech.[3] Google's programs addressed the problem as if it stemmed from sexism and bias in hiring, but Damore's thesis was that other reasons might contribute to the gap as well. He cited research showing that men and women tend to attack problems differently, value work differently, and, largely, think differently. Biological differences, Damore asserted, might result in women choosing not to be software engineers of their own accord. He went on to suggest that making software engineering more collaborative and people-oriented might appeal to women. (Armed with a Ph.D. in biology, Damore seems like he would be at least worth listening to on this subject.)

But Damore's main point was that implicit biases within Google held back discussions and restricted creativity within those trying to solve the gender gap issue. He also called for more ideological diversity, so that people of various political and philosophical stripes would feel comfortable discussing their opinions.

He posted his memo on an internal e-mail listserv. His fellow Googlers weighed in, with many aghast that he would dare explore such territory. Danielle Brown, Google's Vice President of Diversity, Integrity, and Governance (whatever that means), sent a company-wide email dismissing Damore's memo. According to a lawsuit filed later, one manager replied, "Yes, this is 'silencing.' I intend to silence these views."

For the crime of thinking creatively and suggesting that people with different viewpoints be allowed to voice them to prevent closed-minded groupthink, Google fired James Damore.

Think about the place Google has in our lives. If you need a bus schedule, can't remember who sings "So Happy Together," or want to find out where the nearest In-N-Out Burger is, how do you find those things? You Google them. The name of the company has become a common verb. Gmail sends your emails, Google Drive stores your files, and Google Office powers companies you do business with. If you have an Android phone, Google is in your pocket all day, with Google Maps tracking your location. Google Chrome is far and away the most-used web browser. Google Home will adjust your air conditioning or living room lights with a simple voice command. (Oh, and they own YouTube, just to take this discussion full circle.)

Ten or fifteen years ago, Google was essentially the mall directory map that told you where to go on the Internet to find what you needed. Now their products are everywhere, with their hands on almost every aspect of our lives. Most of the services are free to the user, since

Google collects massive amounts of data from us to sell highly targeted ad space. And, as we see from James Damore's experience, Google engages in the same censorship of problematic opinions as we've become used to on college campuses.

Facebook and Twitter—two more networks that put content in front of millions of eyeballs—have their problems with censorship, too. Twitter had to change their algorithm after a Vice News story revealed they were "shadow banning" Republican accounts—in other words, making those accounts harder to find while hiding what they were doing from the account owners and their followers.[4]

The *New York Times* reported that Facebook employees became so fed up with their company's bias that in August 2018 they formed a group called "FB'ers for Political Diversity." Facebook engineer Brian Amerige wrote that the company had become a "political monoculture that's intolerant of different views."

Earlier that month, Facebook, Apple, and Spotify all banned Infowars, Alex Jones's media mini-empire. No matter what you may think of Jones, it's worth asking, "Who's next?" Tomorrow it could be anyone with an unpopular opinion.

$$\oslash$$

PragerU sued Google over the blocked videos—so far unsuccessfully. The first judge ruled that because Google owns the platform, YouTube can restrict, reject, or ban videos as they see fit. They could wield access as a cudgel, dictating who gets to see what and when.

That's not how they like to advertise themselves, though.

The tech behemoths such as Google, Facebook, and Twitter like to position themselves as open forums for discussion. Just as the great thinkers of the past had salons where they could lounge about and come up with great concepts like democracy and freeing slaves, tech companies brag that they offer an unprecedented chance for the world's population to come together and enjoy a free and open exchange of ideas. Technology platforms embrace their role as an equalizing force in the world. Small businesses can sell their products to a worldwide audience. Musicians can play for the world without a record deal. Filmmakers can fill the screen in your pocket without a major Hollywood studio's help.

Colleges talk like this, too. Pick up the recruitment brochure for any school, and you'll read all about how their campus offers incoming students mind-broadening exposure to different views. But when you step onto campus, that claim turns out to be bunk. Professors and administrators only let you explore the views they want you to explore.

Big tech is teeming with young workers who have just stepped out of those colleges that so carefully guard the boundaries of what can and can't be discussed. Is it any wonder that ethos follows them from the university into the wider world? When you search on Google, log onto Facebook, or sign in to Twitter, you get a little slice of campus life: *Join the discussion—as long as you're saying what we want to hear.*

CHAPTER ELEVEN

THAT'S NOT FUNNY! PC KILLS ART

I n the late 1950s, Lenny Bruce launched a stand-up comedy career dedicated to exposing contradictions and hidden truths in society. His profanity-laced tirades against authority figures and (then) commonly held values got him informally banned from appearing on most television shows—and put him in hot water with censors.

In the days before edgy stand-up comedy specials on HBO and Comedy Central became the norm, comedians like Bruce could find a safe haven on college campuses. (Particularly the great George Carlin, who used campus appearances to build a following for his own brand of Bruce-inspired, intellectually challenging humor.)

The fit was perfect: smart, challenging humor meets an audience used to having the reaches of their minds expanded. Given the cultural norms at that point in time, that could mean chemically as well as academically.

Today prominent stand-up comics like Jerry Seinfeld, Chris Rock, and Tim Allen eschew college crowds because of political correctness. Administrators and students have scared them away because a joke that kills on *Jimmy Kimmel Live!* could be deemed a violent microaggression at Trigger Warning U.

As anyone who has tried stand-up comedy can tell you, part of the art is managing your interaction with the crowd. Funny jokes won't cut it if you can't cajole an audience. Sometimes jokes fall flat one night, even if they killed the night before. Sometimes, you say something you think is funny but a crowd's reaction (or lack thereof) will tell you that you stepped over a line. As long as it isn't something truly horrible (like wishing dysentery on Oprah or shouting racial slurs at a heckler, as Michael Richards did years ago), it's not the end of the world. You just have to be able to recover and keep the crowd on your side.

Now let's think about how stand-up plays out on a college campus.

You take the stage, and during your act you say something that doesn't go over great. You can rebound. You cajole the audience and get them back on your side, maybe make fun of yourself a little, and you move on. But wait! If someone is bootlegging your performance with his or her iPhone, maybe your quasi-offensive remark winds up on YouTube with no context. Said video is shared on Twitter and Facebook. By the time you arrive at your next campus gig, there's an army of social justice warriors demanding that your act be shut down. Then no one wants to book you in regular venues or on TV because you're suddenly a "controversial" comic.

Why deal with that headache? Many comics who have a choice are choosing not to.

⊘

In preparation for the *No Safe Spaces* tour, Adam spent time commiserating with some of his fellow comedians. You'd be hard pressed to find a better group to talk about the relationship between art and the culture of political correctness.

Because to be perfectly clear, when we talk about where comedy is going, we're really talking about the future of art at large.

Entertainment may be pop art, but it's still art. Tchaikovsky expressed himself through moving instrumental musical pieces because that's how you expressed your imagination in the culture of his time. That's how you reached people's hearts and minds. If he were alive today, maybe he'd have a limited-run Netflix drama series.

We have already seen political correctness infect all sorts of art. Dennis got to see it first hand when he was invited to guest conduct the Santa Monica Symphony Orchestra in August 2017. His appearance helped the orchestra raise operating funds. But some of the musicians decided to boycott the performance because they disagreed with Dennis's politics. The show was great regardless of the boycott. (Dennis even got to show off his accordion skills.)

When national news outlets picked up the controversy, politically conservative orchestral musicians from across the country contacted

Dennis. Most said they kept their political views under wraps, fearing the consequences should anyone in their own symphony find out.

Art takes many different forms, but there is one constant: good art expands your mind. It makes you think. It can entertain you, too, but if it's good, it makes you a little bit smarter.

For that to happen, you have to be willing to engage with art. In closing down minds, colleges narrow the acceptable range of thought. Art becomes less effective when you tell an artist what he can and can't say, or when you tell an audience what they can and can't like.

Look at jazz, where African rhythms and European melodies merged to create a unique blend of music. It is a distinctly American style—and it never would have worked if you had had people wringing their hands about "cultural appropriation."

Bryan Callen calls this process "idea sex."

You may have seen Callen as Mr. Mellor, the gym teacher on *The Goldbergs*. Or you may remember him as the wedding chapel owner in *The Hangover*. He has also had dramatic roles on shows like HBO's *Oz* and CBS's *CSI: Crime Scene Investigation*. (Adam and Bryan appeared together in the 2011 epic *Division III: Football's Finest*, which was robbed of several Oscars.)

Callen talked to Adam about how exchanges between cultures have made people smarter through an exchange of skills and concepts.

"If you are an Inuit, I had better learn your culture to survive in the Arctic," he said. "But if you come down to LA, bro, you better lose some of your ideas. Like learning how to wear the smell of seal or how to stab a polar bear when it's sleeping. That doesn't work around here. Come take my lesson."

(This is, however, one way to get kicked out of the Los Angeles Zoo.)

Cultures can't mix if you're worried about offending each other. Idea sex, like real sex, often starts with someone saying something borderline inappropriate that another person thinks is sort of interesting or cute, and then there's another comment that's a little "out-there," until finally one party says something that would have gotten them slapped in the face earlier. But by that point, it actually sounds like a pretty good idea.

Comedy, more than any other art form, skirts the edge of what's acceptable in a society and gives us the chance to ponder the unacceptable in a non-threatening way. If you're looking for the proverbial canary in the coal mine to see how the toxicity seeping off campus and into society affects art, look no farther than the main room at the Chuckle Hut.

America is this amazing cultural melting pot. Over three centuries, wave after wave of new citizens have come to our shores, joined our culture... and then turned around and made fun of the next group of immigrants.

Ethnic humor holds a special place in our culture, and it's not because America is a racist cesspool.

Have you ever been at a Christmas party where no one is talking, no one is having fun, and the eggnog isn't kicking in? Then someone walks in wearing a stupid sweater, and maybe you give that guy a little bit of crap for wearing said stupid sweater. You aren't saying he's an idiot—you're just saying he *looks* like an idiot. Everyone laughs, and he laughs, too, because he knows the sweater is a little dumb. Then he gives you some crap back because your sweater isn't so great, either. Everyone takes the jokes in stride, and suddenly everyone's having a good time. Maybe it's the eggnog kicking in, or maybe everyone is lightening up, not taking themselves so seriously, and finding common ground in their differences.

That's what ethnic humor is for America. It's a chance for constituent groups of society to play along with some light ribbing of each other.

When you laugh at someone or something, it can be a sign of superiority. But when everyone is laughing at each other and himself, it can signal equality.

If you don't think comedy has helped society evolve, look at how racial humor has been handled over the years.

During the vaudeville era, traveling stage shows featured white actors in blackface making fun of the perceived inferiorities of black people. The jokes were at the expense of black people. When the audience laughed, they were laughing at black people. That was flat-out racism. That was a white audience laughing because they felt superior.

But racial humor has changed a lot, especially in the last forty or fifty years.

When Archie Bunker made racially insensitive comments to George Jefferson on *All in the Family*, who were we laughing at? We laughed at Archie Bunker. We knew he was wrong, and that's why it was funny. It's the same for Michael Scott, Steve Carrell's character on *The Office*, or for Eric Cartman on *South Park*. We laugh at them for their ignorance. The racists are now the butt of the joke. We view racism as behavior to be ridiculed.

That's important. It forces the audience to think about the racist's mindset in a certain way. It also marks cultural progress. It's also true that stereotypes change. Once upon a time, Mexicans were portrayed as lazy. You couldn't get a laugh with a lazy trope like that, today—and it's not because we've become more politically correct. It's because we've worked around enough Mexican immigrants to see that they're hard-working. The problem is that, eventually, this new, positive stereotype will become offensive, too. Take, for example, the decision to cut the Apu character from *The Simpsons* for being a racist stereotype of Indian-Americans. But what was the stereotype? Arguably, the funniest line the character ever uttered was, "I have been shot eight times this year, and as a result, I almost missed work." If our greatest sin is portraying minorities as hard-working contributors to American society, we should all be proud of that, or at least literate enough that we don't lump today's racial or ethnic humor in with *Birth of a Nation*.

⊘

During our interviews for the *No Safe Spaces* film, Tim Allen told Adam about a time he watched Lenny Bruce at The Purple Onion, one of the Los Angeles comedy clubs of the 1950s and 1960s that served as a launch pad for emerging comic talent. Bruce was performing a particularly powerful and famous bit where he repeatedly said every racial or ethnic slur he could think of.

"I get chills thinking about it; it was so dramatic," Allen said. Breaking down the bit, Allen said the repetition took the edge away from the slurs. "If we say it enough, these words go away."

You might know Tim Allen from his two hit sitcoms based on his stand-up comedy (*Home Improvement* and *Last Man Standing*). You might have heard his voice as Buzz Lightyear in the *Toy Story* movies. You also might know him because between the *Santa Clause* franchise and *Christmas with the Kranks*, you can see his grinning mug during the entirety of December.

But recently the iconic comedian has found himself second-guessing the things he says on stage.

"I'm a little worried about it, a little alarmed about things I cannot say," Allen volunteered. He worries, despite the security he has earned and the success that has proven people find him funny and entertaining. Now, when a joke falls flat with an audience, he wonders whether it's really just a joke falling flat or if he has crossed a line. "It is weird that I'm thinking a little bit."

We can relate. Dennis is on the radio live every day. Adam does live performances of his podcasts across the country. Both are largely unscripted—they require Adam and Dennis to think on their feet and react to what other people say. Obviously, the goals are different. Dennis wants to enlighten, and Adam appeals to your lizard brain instincts for a laugh—but in both cases, they ultimately want you to be entertained.

Unscripted entertainment requires free thought. You can't entertain someone if you live in fear of crossing a line. When Adam is on stage doing his live podcast recordings, that's ninety straight minutes of Adam and his guests. An hour and a half, no commercials, and very few breaks.

Humor is by nature based on negativity. If Adam is on stage and someone asks what he thinks of his mother-in-law, he doesn't reply,

"Megan is a delight, thank you very much." That's not funny, even if Megan is a delight. (She most certainly is, for the record.) If you're in the audience, that's not what you want to hear, either. You want to hear a three-minute riff on all the beef Adam has with his mother-in-law—all about the last time she came over and spoiled the kids or the last time she sparked an argument between Adam and his wife. That is the gut-busting stuff you want.

If you're in the audience, you know it's an exaggeration, but you don't care. It doesn't have to be true to life to be funny. You know that Adam and his mother-in-law aren't constantly at each other's throats. How could they be? After all, Megan is a delight.

⊘

When we talked to him for the *No Safe Spaces* film, comedian Adam Schulz insisted that humor can't exist without free speech.

"Give me a place with no free speech, and I'll show you unfunny people," Schulz told us. "Russian comedy is: There's a doll, and then you open it, and then there is little doll. And then—wait for it—you open that little doll, and there is an even smaller doll."

"That's no-free-speech comedy."

(Naturally, we apologize to all the Russians who may be offended by this example of cultural appropriation.)

⊘

There are times when you can push an envelope too far. During his conversation with Adam, comedian Bryan Callen shared how he learned that lesson the hard way. Early in his career he jokingly used the word "faggot" in front of an openly gay drama teacher.

The teacher might have kicked Callen out of his class. Or he might have taken the chance to publicly shame Callen and make him an outcast among the theater community (with whatever professional implications came along with that). Instead he took Callen aside and explained the history of violence associated with the word. The drama teacher told Callen how the pejorative had been used by hateful mobs who beat gays to death at a time when society was less tolerant of homosexuality.

The conversation with his teacher affected Callen.

"When he described it that way," Callen told Adam, "I suddenly went, 'I don't want to use that word anymore.'"

The calm, reasonable discussion made Callen think about people in his audience. What if his language reminded them of their own run-ins with violence? The guy on stage with a microphone wants everyone to have a good time, so why remind them of their most painful experiences?

"If you couch it that way, and let people make a choice," Callen reasoned, "If you educate people about the word, I think language is always changed organically."

"My problem," Callen added, "is when it's imposed as an ideology."

Free thought and free speech allow us to have those conversations—if we are patient and assume the best about each other. Educational discussions can lead to real progress.

Callen could have been prevented from using that word with hard-and-fast rules about what people can and can't say. But then how would he have learned anything? Rules like that create an artificial, superficial politeness. It's like cheating on an eye test—you can get the answers right, but it doesn't mean you should be driving a school bus.

(We would like to apologize to any visually impaired people we may have offended with that last sentence. On second thought, we'll just edit that out of the braille version of the book.)

Why not let these conversations happen? Why restrict what people can and can't say or do?

It all comes down to power.

No one can control what other people think (barring intense psychological torture—and really, who has the time for that?). But if you're in a position of authority, you can control what other people do and say. You can exert power that way. You can tell people what they should think by telling them how to live.

Look at smoking.

In the 1960s, you could smoke in a restaurant. Then, under the guise of public health, some anti-smoking activists and their allies in local governments decided there shouldn't be so much smoking in restaurants, and they created smoking sections. Smoking patrons had to get up, grab their plates, and move over to their new little corner of the restaurant. Then smoking was banned except at the bar. When that wasn't good enough, the smokers had to move outside. But the smokers were too close to the building, so they were asked to move again, down to the park. Then smoking was banned in the park.

So smokers stopped smoking and instead started using the little vapor things—just water and nicotine. Then those got restricted, too. If the anti-smoking people were so concerned about people inhaling tar fumes, they would love vaping. It would be the greatest thing ever because it keeps people from smoking.

But the anti-smoking people aren't really just anti-smoking. They are pro-telling-you-what-to-do. They are pro-power. So it doesn't matter what rules you comply with, there will always be more. There's no end game, no finish line. It's an addiction.

Like smoking.

The alternative to this type of heavy-handed power is the empowerment of free thought and the knowledge that comedy—and, in fact, all art—can be used to expand your thinking.

"There is another kind of power that this country was built on," Bryan Callen told Adam. "That's the power to awe."

He is right. No one can force you think something, but an artist—whether they work with a microphone, a paintbrush, a pen, or a camera—can make you think.

There is a much greater power in that.

"That's the kind of power that causes you to look up and not be able to take your eyes off the person," Callen continued. "Look up and want to be like that person. Look up and want to be close to that person. Look up and want to hear that person because they fill you with the possibility that they [can] teach you what your potential is. They disturb you, and they change your mind.

"The great comics do that."

⊘

When Lenny Bruce died of an apparent drug overdose in 1966, he was a shell of his former groundbreaking self. And it wasn't just the drugs.

When Bruce started out, he was too edgy for television. As he gained notoriety, he became too edgy for local authorities, who used anti-obscenity laws to shut down clubs at which he was performing. The heavy hand of the law forced comedy club owners to make a choice: book Lenny Bruce and face police raids, or don't book him and don't get harassed by cops.

Bruce had trouble finding work. And his art suffered.

"Eventually, Lenny became unfunny," recalled Tim Allen, who saw Bruce at the height of his abilities and then watched his career spiral. "He got exhausted from being beleaguered by the law."

Heavy-handed censorship turned the godfather of stand-up comedy into a bitter, humorless, and, worst of all, less thought-provoking version of himself. The censorship of political correctness may be less obvious, but its damage stretches further.

When modern-day Lenny Bruces hang up their microphones, we all miss out.

EXTRA CREDIT: ANDREW SCHULZ ON FREE SPEECH AND COMEDY

When stand-up comedian, podcaster, and MTV2 personality Andrew Schulz was interviewed for *No Safe Spaces*, this is what he had to say about the role free speech plays in comedy:

Free speech is a very unnatural thing. That's why it took us thousands of years to get there, right? It's not like in the Bible there is anywhere written, "Hey, you can say whatever you want," right? It's just written all the things you can't say pretty much.

The second any human gets power they immediately limit what other people can say to them. That's just what you do.

○

I never understood comics that, like, have jokes about things we all agree about because, if you and I agree on something, why are we talking? Like, you're wasting my breath. You know what I mean? "It's hot out." Yep, thanks for that scintillating tidbit about the weather today, Justin…

I know if I write a joke about something you agree with you'll laugh because it's a tribal thing…. Now if you're a good comic the jokes should not be about how bad Trump is. The joke should be about things he does that are right. That's the challenge.

○

Free speech is still free, it just costs more. You know what I mean? You're still free to say whatever you want but the price is raised. Now if you have a difference of opinion you're immediately a bigot, you're a Nazi, you're a snowflake, or whatever. You just get labeled.

I never understood this in my whole life why the expectations for comedians are so high. Like, most comedians are high school graduates that sleep on couches, and we have the same expectations as Congressmen. Like, give me the expectations of a gangster rapper....

The more I shouldn't be able to make something funny, the harder I will try because that's the gratification. That's the intellectual satisfaction. It's like making a crowd laugh at a joke that you're pandering to them for, right, that's like [having sex with] a hooker. You don't have game.... But if you want to get the Playboy Bunny, the Victoria Secret model, you got to put the work in.

⊘

It's very simple. The more I can say, the funnier I'm going to be.

So free speech, here's the thing. Free speech is like a nipple ring, right? I had this girl I was dating, and she had got a nipple piercing, and she would always be playing with it, and I was like, yo, this girl is a freak.... And she's like, no, no, no, I have to rotate it or else it will close.... "

You have to push the boundaries or else it closes, and every little bit that they take away is the skin closing on that nipple ring, and a nipple ring is fun when you can move it around. It's not fun when it's part of the nipple, right, and in a lot of countries it started out with this idea where you could say whatever you want, right. Shit, Cuba, Castro went in there like, yeah, we got to liberate everybody and then some people were like, "I kind of like America," and he was like, "Chill with that shit," right. That nipple ring got a little skin grafted around it, and now it's not moving at all. So free speech is a nipple ring, man. There we go.

$\bigcirc$

It's a weird concept to understand but you have to make a choice a lot of times. What is the cost of free speech, and what's the cost of censorship? I think the cost of censorship is always higher. The cost of free speech is you might hear some things that you don't like. The cost of censorship is you might not get to like things.... I'll put up with whatever comes with free speech because I know the evil that is censorship.

$\bigcirc$

These kids that equate speech to violence, that could be the dumbest thing I've ever heard in my entire life. You know what you use when you don't want to be violent? Speech. And you know what you use when you can no longer speak? Violence.... You want people speaking bad things because it means they're not blowing people up.... The second you stop speech what do I have left? I got to beat you up.... You don't want violence, let people talk.

CHAPTER TWELVE

POISONING OUR POLITICS

Coming up in the New York City comedy scene, Dave Rubin thought of himself as on the political left.

Hailing from Long Island, Rubin started out as most comics do, grabbing time at open mic nights and eventually being featured at various clubs in the city. After interning at *The Daily Show*, he and a few fellow comics started a subversive, local, public-access version of the mock-news program. They called it *The Anti-Show* and filmed it secretly at NBC's New York headquarters. Later he started a handful of comedy podcasts, one of which (*The Six Pack*) became so popular on iTunes that Sirius XM picked up the show.

Rubin's success and his liberal sensibility led him to branch out from comedy into more serious fare. He launched his own talk show, *The Rubin Report*, as part of The Young Turks network.

Founded in 2002, The Young Turks (TYT) grew out of skepticism about the post-9/11 War on Terror and opposition to then-President George W. Bush. Appearing on various cable and radio networks, TYT really hit its stride when it became one of the first successful, fully-online media ventures, offering YouTube videos and podcasts. The Young Turks tapped into growing anti-war sentiment and became a key contributor to a rising progressive movement.

Rubin counted himself as a member of its ranks until sometime after he saw neuroscientist Sam Harris on a 2014 episode of *Real Time with Bill Maher*. Citing data from Pew surveys, Harris talked about how some Muslims were Islamists who saw violent jihad as the avenue for social change, and how the Muslim world was largely backward on human rights that Americans take for granted. This sparked fellow panelist Ben Affleck, noted actor and non-scientist, to characterize Harris as a bigot.

"It's gross; it's racist," Affleck averred.

Affleck's remark puzzled Rubin because Harris's points were from studies and surveys rather than the conjecture that typically passes for analysis in interview shows. Then, over the next few days, he watched social media pick up the discussion. Criticism of Harris and Maher was nearly universal, coming even from TYT founder Cenk Uygur.

"Suddenly, the onus was on them to prove that they weren't racist," Rubin said, calling the barrage a "feeding frenzy." He found it especially jarring knowing that Maher regularly takes liberal stances—opposing wars, standing up for free speech, and supporting equal rights for women and minorities. Supposed liberals' piling on an ally for fact-based commentary seemed flat-out wrong.

Rubin started noticing those he had thought were his ideological *simpaticos* work themselves into what he saw as a "constant hysteria" at every opportunity for controversy. Some people seemed to take particular joy in working themselves into a lather over anything on Fox News. Most disturbingly, the merits of what a pundit or newsmaker said—or even the actual content of their comments—seemed to matter less than the perception. Someone like Harris, who wanted to argue about the consequence of a factual data point, was attacked for even bringing up the fact.

Then came the 2015 attack on *Charlie Hebdo*, the French humor magazine. In response to cartoons depicting the Muslim prophet Muhammad, two radical Islamist brothers burst into the magazine's office and shot the place up, murdering twelve and wounding eleven. (Previously, a 2011 depiction of Muhammed had inspired a bombing attempt.)

Rubin watched as the Left—rather than condemn the attackers—chastised satirists for poking fun at religious symbols in ways that might offend some people.

Rubin still counts himself a liberal: he's pro-choice, pro-public education, and pro-gay marriage. In fact, he's gay and married himself. You would be hard pressed to find someone who is a better example of what the Left claims to support.

Intellectually, however, Rubin has left the Left.

⊘

If people are leaving campus to ruin America's businesses, technology, and art, why not ruin politics while they're at it?

When we say politics, we're not just talking about the politicians themselves, but also about the news media that covers politics. The two are almost inseparable. Politicians play to the media, the media reacts, and politicians react to the coverage and play to the media—it's a never-ending, closed-loop system. And it's not of recent development. Whether you're a devoted student of American history or simply enjoy tooling around suburbia in your minivan listening to the *Hamilton* soundtrack, you know that the press and the politicians have had a weird relationship since George Washington's administration.

The intolerant Left that dominates campuses has found its way into both the government and the entities that report on government, thus poisoning the entire feedback loop.

This trend became obvious when President Barack Obama proposed sweeping reforms to health care in 2009. Many of his ideas involved more federal government control over the health care system, an idea Republicans and conservatives had opposed vociferously since the previous Democratic President, Bill Clinton, had proposed it in 1993. During the debate over what became known as Obamacare and in the years since, defenders of the law have been happy to inject race into the discourse. Isn't it funny, they'll tell you, that Republicans are opposing this law proposed by a black President? Yes, it's odd that Republicans are opposing ideas that they have opposed for a quarter century. It's a real mystery why they would still stand against the same policies that they opposed when a white Southerner put them before Congress.

For eight years, any opposition to Obama's proposals was chalked up to racism—just as, for decades, any opposition to welfare programs got chalked up to hating some group or another. Oppose welfare dependency? You hate the poor. Object to abortion? You must hate women. Don't think the federal government should subsidize the Museum of History's Greatest Left-Handers in East Bumblescum, Nebraska, exhibit? You're a Right-wing bigot. (See what we did there?)

The leftists in politics have adopted the same mindset as their pals in academia. They so deeply believe in their own correctness on every issue that they can't imagine anyone else coming to a different conclusion.

You might oppose entitlement programs because poverty levels have remained nearly unchanged since President Lyndon Johnson declared his "War on Poverty" five decades ago. (In fact, given the way poverty had been trending downward in the twentieth century up to that point, you sort of have to give poverty the win there, right?) You might have scientific reasons for opposing abortion. You might oppose Obamacare because the past decade has seen a spike in health insurance premiums. But to the Left, these reasons are just how you justify your hatred of the poor, women, and black people.

This poison has been especially pervasive since the 2016 election.

Hillary Clinton's supporters thought they had the election in the bag. They had been running their victory lap since August, and election night was supposed to be a formality. Donald Trump had spent most of the previous year and a half saying things that drew unfavorable media coverage. Election prediction sites gave Clinton somewhere around a 98 percent chance of victory—in fact, critics roasted FiveThirtyEight's Nate Silver for giving Trump as much as a 1-in-3 chance of winning.

When Trump won, the tears at Clinton's aborted victory party were not just tears of sadness, but also of disbelief. And rather than come together with their fellow Americans after the election and try to move forward, the Left allowed the wound to fester.

During the campaign, left-leaning pundits (and some right-leaning pundits too, to be fair) wrung their hands at Trump's vague answers when he was asked whether he would accept the results of the election if he didn't win. But then almost immediately after the election, Trump opponents insisted he was "not my President." Online organizers tried to encourage members of the Electoral College to flip their votes to give the election to Clinton instead. (They did not—marking the first time in decades a college didn't obey far-left talking points.)

During the campaign, Clinton and her allies had expressed fear that Trump's rhetoric would spur right-wing violence. At Trump's inauguration, left-wing protesters set a car on fire.

Celebrities hobnobbed happily with President Obama, and no one thought anything of it. When Steve Harvey and Kanye West met with Trump to discuss issues that the president has authority over, they received backlash from left-wing commentators. Critics lambaste those who "normalize" Trump, as if he is an outlier in American society, despite winning a presidential election.

The most vociferous opponents to Trump call themselves "the Resistance." You know where they borrowed that idea from? It comes from France in the 1940s, where it was the term used for those fighting Nazi occupation. When you hear someone talking about "resisting" the Trump administration, they are likening the 2016 election to the Wehrmacht that blitzkrieged its way over the French countryside.

That seems a little over the top, doesn't it?

Television pundits, columnists, and other commentators love to use the phrase, "in this political environment" as shorthand for the current polarization in American politics. It's true that neither political party is dominant right now. Four of the last five presidential elections have been decided by smaller-than-5-percent margins in the popular vote, and four of the last five mid-term elections have seen a shift in party control of at least one chamber of Congress. With things so evenly divided, a power shift is always just an election away. You can understand why someone might try to create that "constant hysteria" Dave Rubin described—with suggestions that their political opponents are the modern equivalents of Nazis.

This technique is especially effective when the political figures stoking that hysteria have such an eager accomplice in the news media.

⊘

Sharyl Attkisson has won awards for her critical thinking. Mark has been a fan of hers since her days at CNN in the early 1990s. He really wanted her to be a part of the *No Safe Spaces* film because she's relentless and fair—and doesn't take sides.

As an investigative reporter with CBS through the 1990s and 2000s, she worked on the type of story you imagine when you hear the word "journalism." Her reporting has pushed back on official narratives from big business and big government alike, and she's done it by talking to people, doing her research, and compiling information. At a time when most so-called news programs present quasi-entertainment in the form of bickering panelists spouting off opinions, Attkisson has painstakingly forged a career from fact-finding.

But over the past two decades, she has seen an increase in fact-phobia.

"To me, the red flag as a reporter was when interests started intervening and trying to censor stories entirely," Attkisson told us.

She started seeing the trend in the early 2000s while investigating the nascent anti-vaccination movement. Some fringe parents groups were peddling evidence that vaccinations were a cause of medical conditions such as autism. Attkisson wanted to know more about their claims, but drug companies didn't even want to talk about them. Rather than offering a quote or rebutting the "anti-vaxxer" claims, Attkisson said, pharmaceutical spokespeople threatened to approach her bosses in the news division or appeal to the corporate higher-ups to spike the story.

"I was bewildered" by the pharmaceutical industry's reaction, she recalled. "They should want to be heard in a story, and they should want to debate." Many of the links between vaccinations and illnesses have been debunked, which makes the industry's hostility to the discussion even more self-damaging.

"It's led to this underground movement," said Attkisson, "where you're controversialized if you even ask a logical or rational question about medicine."

This issue shows the risk of shutting down discussion, added Attkisson. "You're left to form your own conclusions. And, of course, that leaves all kinds of conclusions that may be way out there and wrong and farfetched."

If you want to see how a story like this should play out, picture a backyard cookout with your kids. The sun is shining, it's warm but not too hot, and there isn't a cloud in the sky. You are at the grill, flipping burgers and occasionally swigging from an ice-cold bottle of beer. It would be perfect, except for the kid who won't go play wiffle ball with the others. Instead he's at your hip, begging for a sip of your brew.

Here's the right way to handle this: You grin a little bit, turn to the kid, and say, "Sure!" You offer the kid the tiniest of sips. You stifle your laugh as his face contorts into a prune. "Yuck!" the kid exclaims, and you are left in peace.

But let's say instead that you respond with a flat, "No." Then you have to deal with the "Aw, come on!" and "Just a little sip!" appeals process. By the time the little pest has finally figured out that no means no, you've burned the burgers.

Attkisson sees government officials, corporations, and even her media colleagues choosing the burned burger route. That's bad enough when those groups are in the right, but it's especially troubling when they might be in the wrong. Shutting down other viewpoints ensures that audiences won't have an opportunity to hear and consider their merits. It's easier to win a debate when your opponent isn't allowed to talk.

Just like with college faculty, administration, and left-leaning students who want to see universal acceptance for their own ideology, this issue boils down to control. Politicians seek to stamp out any discussion for fear that voters might reasonably draw conclusions different from their own. If you can't control people's decision-making process, you can at least try to scare them away from differing viewpoints.

Have you noticed how suddenly every election is "the most important election of our lifetime"? How many of these have we lived through by now? Either we exist at the fulcrum of the history of democracy, or it's all bunk from people trying to scare you. We'll go out on a limb and say it's door number two.

If you wanted to see how the leftists' campaign to shut up their opponents affects politics, you got a clear example in 2018 when the echoes of Title IX-mandated campus judicial boards reverberated through Brett Kavanaugh's Supreme Court confirmation hearings. The process hit a roadblock with Dr. Christine Blasey Ford's allegations that Kavanaugh had sexually assaulted her at party when they both were in high school. Ford had originally made the allegations in an anonymous letter that was later leaked to the press, notably without her consent. But it made for great TV, so the reporters didn't mind. Whatever leftist leaked the accusation clearly hoped that Kavanaugh, confronted with this shaming story at the height of the #MeToo era, would slink off under a rock—or that President Trump could be pressured into withdrawing his nomination.

As the Senate Judiciary Committee grappled with this allegation, two more accusers emerged. One alleged Kavanaugh had exposed himself to her at a party—but she was dubious about whether it was actually Kavanaugh or someone else. Another, Julie Swetnick, released a vague statement placing Kavanaugh at parties where gang rapes had occurred.

But Swetnick's testimony fell apart when witnesses failed to corroborate her story and she contradicted her sworn statements in an NBC interview.

But as when colleges adjudicate sexual harassment and assault cases, the narrative was more important than the facts. To the Democrats on the Senate Judiciary Committee, supporting Kavanaugh was tantamount to turning a cold shoulder on all sexual assault survivors.

No wonder it resonates when President Trump complains about "fake news."

Attkisson left CBS News in 2014 after over twenty years with the network. Later she wrote the book *Stonewalled: One Reporter's Fight for Truth Against the Forces of Obstruction, Intimidation, and Harassment in Obama's Washington.* In the book she offered sharp criticism of the higher-ups at CBS News, who she said declined to give enough coverage to controversies during the Obama administration.

A good journalist, according to Attkisson, has to think critically. This becomes especially important when everyone else seems to be thinking and saying the same thing. Reporters should be suspicious of even their own biases.

It's intellectually rewarding to have your own theories refuted, according to Attkisson: "When you seek the facts, and dig a little bit, and listen to people who know, maybe your mind is changed by the facts on the ground."

That's the job of the journalist. It's a difficult job, and one at which too many are currently failing because of an inability to adopt that inquisitive mindset. By expunging free thought from campuses, our colleges and universities are creating both news makers and news consumers ill equipped to process differing viewpoints, ponder questions, and divine their own conclusions.

⊘

Dave Rubin has held hundreds of conversations, if not more, on *The Rubin Report*, sitting across from newsmakers, creators, and deep thinkers in a simply furnished studio with an exposed brick backdrop subtly harkening back to his roots in stand-up comedy.

But away from the lights and cameras, during a recent conversation at a bar with a politically progressive childhood friend, he ran straight into the buzzsaw of the leftists' political narrative.

Rubin had engaged politically with this friend before, and they frequently disagreed. Their conversations always ended amicably, and they would wind up talking family or playing basketball.

But this time when Rubin tried to talk family, his friend insisted on jumping right into politics. After a few tense exchanges, Rubin asked his friend, "Do you think it's possible that I believe what I believe as much as you believe what you believe?"

No, the friend replied.

Frustrated, Rubin paid the check and left.

The Left's refusal to grant individuals agency over their own philosophy doesn't stop at the bar stools in Rubin's old stomping ground. Smearing opponents as homophobic, Islamophobic, xenophobic, racist, sexist, bigoted, or otherwise misguided is becoming as common off campus in as it already is in the identity politics that dominate higher education. Leftists reduce people to their membership in groups based on superficial characteristics like race, gender, or sexual orientation. Those characteristics are assumed to determine what people believe, and how they vote.

"This is actually the essence of prejudice, really, because 'prejudice' means to prejudge," Rubin told us. "This is the reverse of everything that Martin Luther King, Jr. wanted."

Because identity politics is powered by victimhood, it creates self-perpetuating divisions in society, according to Rubin—even as America becomes increasingly equal. Rubin points to the fight for same-sex marriage. After decades of fighting on various levels of government, the gay community couldn't experience relief over the Supreme Court ruling mandating states to recognize gay marriages.

"In an odd way," Rubin observed, "they've become addicted to the pain." The pain is where some members of the community derive their self-worth, so they must find something else over which to be aggrieved.

Yet even as the Left waves their rainbow flags for diversity based on characteristics, they refuse to acknowledge individuals' rights to think what they want. If you thought they were bad on freedom of speech, they're even worse on freedom of religion. Just ask Jack Phillips, the Colorado baker who had to fight his way to the Supreme Court because he refused to bake a cake for a gay wedding. Until he got to the highest Court in America, every lower court and commission he appeared before told him his religious opposition to gay marriage was irrelevant—he would have to bake a cake for a ceremony he didn't believe in. The Little Sisters of the Poor's opposition to paying for birth control forced them to fight *their* way to the Supreme Court. By the way, if you do have to fight your way anywhere, it's a good idea to have nuns in your corner with their rulers of fury. Little Sisters of the Poor? More like Little Sisters of Your Poor Knuckles.

Dave Rubin doesn't talk on college campuses much, but when he does, he tends to get invited by conservative and libertarian groups—organizations he tends to disagree with on many political issues. But if he doesn't find common ground with them on every issue position, he finds the conversations more respectful and pleasant.

"We can agree to disagree," Rubin said. "There's simply none of that on the left anymore."

The heightened level of scrutiny of politically incorrect behavior is a problem that extends into our daily life, according to Rubin. He worries about a future when average people are afraid to engage in discussion on social media for fear that a comment could be later deemed insensitive, go viral, and force a publicity-averse employer to cut the poster loose rather than deal with the outrage machine.

Rubin's advice: "Keep talking."

"The best thing you can do is not only say who you are and what you believe in, but also sometimes realize that you have to pick a moment to fight," he told us. "For me, this [moment] is the one. I don't even know that I picked it. Maybe it picked me."

EXTRA CREDIT: VAN JONES ON GETTING ALONG

Commentator, author, and Obama administration veteran Van Jones stopped by Adam's *Take a Knee* podcast and talked about how Americans can find common ground in today's political climate:

I grew up in the rural South, edge of a small town. Because my dad had been born in segregation and poverty, he joined the military. When everybody else was running out, my dad ran in to get out of poverty. Put himself through college....

He worked with my mom to put me and my twin sister through college. And basically he got our entire family out of poverty just through sheer effort and force of his will. Also the NAACP had to sue our county for him to be able to become a principal. They gave him the worst junior high school in our county, and he turned it into the best in the state. So my dad was just one of these guys just kind of hard to stop. I was his first and only son. When I got accepted to Yale for Law School, I decided I wanted to be a civil rights guy. And I wanted to kind of be a give-back-guy like my dad had been. And wound up working on every issue you can imagine, tough urban environments. And I really learned from my dad that the liberals get it wrong, the conservatives get it wrong. If you're really trying to deal with tough, urban issues you got to be the most conservative person and the liberal person at the same time.

You got to be a liberal to fight for these programs and for some real opportunity, but then once the kids get the opportunity you gotta be a drill sergeant. You gotta be the most conservative human ever born to get the young people to show up on time, to do what's right, to take responsibility. So we need each other.... That kind of just common sense seems to have completely escaped the country. I don't know where it went. But it's not available anymore in either party.

⊘

If you're a Democrat you have to pretend that Hillary Clinton is a walking god who's never done anything wrong. Or, if you're a Republican, Donald Trump is doing a fantastic job, he couldn't improve in any way. We're flunking kindergarten here at this point.

You wouldn't want your kids to have that kind of attitude about their friends or about their school, about their neighborhood.... I'm a proud progressive. Left side of Pluto. But I work with Newt Gingrich on opioid issues, on criminal justice issues, because some of these things are just commonsense American issues. While we're fighting about stuff we're never going to agree on, we forget that 80 percent of stuff we do agree on, we can get something done about....

It turns out that two things can be true at the same time: that you can have an unfair society (which I think that we do), and that you shouldn't use that as an excuse not to be world-class excellent in every way you can possibly be.

That's how I was raised.... When my father died, the picture that they put on the funeral program is my father standing in front of Yale Law School with his hands in the air just so proud that his son had been able to get there, considering he grew up literally in a shotgun shack. Now did he have to go up against unfair things? Did the NAACP have to come to our county and literally file a lawsuit to get him a shot to be a principal? Yes. But once he got that shot, the lawyers went home, and he had to produce kids who could go on to high school and to college. And he did that.

That's the country that you live in. It's not fair. [There's] never been a fair country in the world, but you got a better shot here than any place else. Let's work hard on the fairness part, that's the liberal part. Let's also work hard on the personal responsibility and excellence part, which has now become a conservative thing.

And it's definitely nuts to me that we split it this way.

$\oslash$

I think that most Americans right now—I don't care if you're a red state or blue state, black, white, Latino, whatever, I think people feel very insecure right now.

I think there's a lot of change that's just coming... changes in technology, changes in gender roles, demographic changes, geopolitical changes. And people are insecure. The question is, are we gonna turn to each other and realize, we got the genius of every kind of human ever born in one country, we can figure it out? Or are we going to turn on each other and just start fighting like idiots?…The dividers have a very simple thing: just blame the other side. Take no responsibility, and you can get a following. But the problem is you won't have a country if you keep doing that.

And so we've got to figure out, okay fine, some stuff we're not gonna agree on, [we] can fight on that stuff. But you got to start identifying stuff we can actually work on, like criminal justice, like education, like this addiction crisis and get some progress somewhere, or we're going to be in deep trouble.

⊘

We are trying to do something that is almost impossible. If you look at human history, we've got every kind of human being ever born in one country. Every faith, every gender, every sexuality, every kind of person in one country. And we mostly get along. Nobody points that out: we mostly get along. You know other countries, they got two groups, and they're in a civil war. And they'll never stop fighting. We got like thirty-nine languages spoken in the L.A. public schools. And we mostly get along. So where it gets hard, takes real work.… you gotta listen to each other. And we don't have to agree, we can disagree. That's democracy. Dictatorship, you can't disagree. Democracy, you get to disagree. It's called freedom. But you don't have to disrespect and disregard. And it's become fashionable now to not just disagree, which we've always done, but to disrespect and disregard.

CHAPTER THIRTEEN

WHAT CAN PARENTS DO?

When Professor Jordan Peterson visited Adam's warehouse/ podcast studio to talk about the culture on college campuses, the subject of the *Sleeping Beauty* fairy tale surprisingly came up. There's nothing quite like a couple of dudes, surrounded by classic cars, kicking back, and shooting the bull about Disney princess movies. There was clearly a real testosterone overload that day; it was toxic masculinity in all of its glory.

As all of our gentlemen readers surely remember, Princess Aurora (that's Sleeping Beauty's real name) was the only child of a king and queen who had been trying to have a kid for a while (Disney cut out that part, which is probably for the best). When she finally came along, her parents were so thrilled that they threw a kingdom-wide christening celebration, inviting everyone in their realm—except for the evil, antlered fairy Maleficent.

"She's maliciousness. She's evil, and she's the negative element of life," explained Peterson. The king and queen don't want her anywhere near their daughter "because who the hell wants evil and tragedy at their daughter's christening?"

What happens to Princess Aurora? As the story goes, the bad element crashes the party and hurts their daughter just the same. One evil enchantment later, Aurora is destined for a century of sleep. She'll be blind, deaf, and dumb to the world. She'll remain forever sixteen—until Prince Charming comes along to break the spell.

Peterson sees a counterintuitive lesson for today's parents in the story.

"You have to invite the terrible thing into your child's life. And if you don't do that, you weaken them," said Peterson.

As we have already seen, many of the problems on campus are rooted in pre-college family life. Helicopter parents stand over their kids, hovering, with a squeeze bottle of Purell ready so little Johnny or Suzy can be protected from evil germs. Bulldozer parents clear the way, moving aside obstacles so little McKenzie or Anderson has a clear path to success.

Like the king and the queen who tried to sneak a christening past Maleficent, these well-meaning folks think they can eliminate the bad from their kids' lives. Really, all they can do is delay it. And in trying to protect their children, they actually weaken them.

Human muscles require resistance to function properly and get stronger. If you lift heavy weights, you get stronger over time. In low gravity, astronauts' muscles will atrophy. (If you ever want to take an astronaut's wallet, wait until he returns from an extended stay on the International Space Station. He won't be able to stop you.) Or maybe you've heard the trope about the man who tried to help the butterfly out of his cocoon. It turns out that depriving the butterfly of the struggle to get out results in small, shriveled wings. The man thought he was helping the butterfly, but he was really killing it. The human mind works the same way—it requires argument, discussion, and debate to become smarter.

Yes, clearing the path for your daughter will help her succeed in the short term. But empty successes will weaken your kids to the point of causing them long-term problems. We talked in previous chapters about how colleges and universities do the same thing, and how they often take their cues from the expectations parents have established.

Fixing higher education starts with parents.

Parents have kids for eighteen years before sending them off to college. That's eighteen years before the professors start filling their heads with notions of privilege and identity politics. And it's eighteen years before a guest speaker or an election exposes them to mild disagreements that send them to a safe room complete with coloring books and Play-Doh (with world music playing in the background).

College exposes them to four years of that drivel. If you're a parent, you have eighteen years to toughen up your kid before it happens. Let's get to work.

$$\oslash$$

Children need to fail.

They cannot appreciate what it takes to succeed until they fail—until they pour their effort into something only to experience the gut-punch of realizing that it wasn't enough. You definitely don't learn as much from getting things right all the time.

Think about that old cliché about a hot stove. You can tell your toddler daughter (for example) not to touch the stove until you're blue in the face. She will still want to touch it. Actually, telling her not to touch it makes her want to touch it even more. Putting safety guards and baby gates all around it will protect her precious little hand, but it won't really teach her anything. But when she touches the hot surface and yanks her hand back, yowling in pain, she finally understands your instructions. She will have a frame of reference next time you tell her, "Don't touch that, it's hot."

Thanks for the lesson, hot stove.

Failure is the first step in a lesson about responsibility. When a child gets a bad grade on a test, it's a sign that she needs to study more. When your Little League all-star strikes out, it's a sign he needs to practice more. In the parlance of our times, it's a "teachable moment."

Children need to learn that if they don't prepare for life's events, they risk failure. When they're kids, that means studying before the big test or practicing before the big game. When they reach adulthood, it could mean saving for a house or ensuring that they have medical insurance in case their appendix needs to be removed. Better to feel the sting of failure when the stakes are low.

A corollary to letting kids fail: embrace (or at least accept) the messiness of childhood.

Too often, parents try to create an anti-microbial, antiseptic bubble around their kids. They have little dispensers of hand sanitizer everywhere—at the kitchen counter, in the console of the minivan, in mom's purse, in dad's European-style, carry-all satchel (a.k.a. man purse)—lest their child have an evil germ land on his or her precious hand.

This effort is doomed. Kids are petri dishes of filth. Without adult supervision, they pass around spores willy-nilly, like crop dusters of disease. They'll swap half-eaten sandwiches, share juice boxes, and high-five each other with snot-smeared hands. And you know what? They've been acting like that for thousands of years, and the human race still exists. Why? Because biology tells us that exposure to small amounts of bad stuff makes us stronger. Our bodies learn how to handle it. That is how vaccines work—you get a small, manageable amount of a disease to build a natural immunity. Recent studies have shown that the effects of peanut allergies can be reduced by introducing low levels of peanut dust. (Was peanut dust something George Washington Carver came up with?)

In the not-too-distant past, parents would use biology to their advantage. Chicken pox is easier to deal with when you're younger. If one child came down with chicken pox, parents would make sure all the brothers and sisters got exposed. Other parents would intentionally make their own children play alongside the infected. Kids would go through a rough week, and that would be it—no more chicken pox. Ever. Once they built up their immunity, they would never again have to worry about it. Sometimes good parenting looks a little bit like germ warfare, at least in the short run.

Just as parents need to help their children build up their immunity, they also need to cultivate their independence.

But today giving kids autonomy can be (incredibly) controversial. In 2008, Lenore Skenazy wrote an article for the *New York Sun* titled, "Why I Let My 9-Year-Old Ride the Subway Alone." You can imagine the story. You can also probably imagine how it was received. One commenter called the writer the "World's Worst Mom."

In 2015, suburban Washington, D.C., parents Danielle and Alexander Meitiv were investigated by child protective services for the crime of letting their children walk home alone from a local park.

In early 2018 Utah actually passed a law allowing parents to let their kids walk home from school, go to a store alone, or sit in a car by themselves while a parent runs into a store.

Good for Utah, but why does there need to be a law to let this happen? What busybodies are peeking out from behind living room drapes, dropping the dime on parents because their kids are walking home from a park? If we want our society's children to take more responsibility in their own lives, we need to start by letting parents parent. No one knows your kid like you do. If you think your kid is smart enough to cross the street, it should be up to you to let him or her do so. Taking parental responsibility out of parents' hands only results in bad parenting.

What happens when you live in a Purell bubble? Eventually there's a breach, and things that your body would have toughened itself up against suddenly become dangerous.

We aren't saying that your next family vacation should be to the remains of Reactor Number Four at Chernobyl, or that your kids bring smallpox blankets to their next sleepover. Just give their growing immune systems a chance to do (and get better at) their job.

⊘

Youth sports offer a good, relatively safe way to instill the taste of failure—if they're done the right way. (Obviously, we don't mean soccer games where no one keeps score so that "everyone wins!" That is the opposite of helpful.)

In high school, Dennis was a member of the Yeshiva Flatbush basketball team. At 6'4"—in high school, mind you—Dennis was the tallest Jew in New York. He made the team by default and rode the bench. That was just fine, since he didn't even care for basketball.

"Air" Prager made his Madison Square Garden debut in the last minute of an exhibition game, when his coach decided it was mathematically impossible to win. Since Dennis had not been expecting to have his number called, he turned to a teammate asking which basket their team was shooting on. The teammate wouldn't tell him. After a jump ball, Dennis ran to the opposing basket (leading the closest ref to ask if he was "some kind of schmuck"), then spent the subsequent fifty-seven seconds until the final buzzer trying to look busy and avoid the ball.

(That is not exactly a success story about youth sports. However, it is a great story, and it gave us an excuse to use the word "schmuck" in the book.)

Adam, on the other hand, started playing Pop Warner football when he was seven. It was his own idea, after seeing a flyer outside his house. Football gave him an outlet, which his lethargic parents couldn't provide, for his youthful hyperactivity (and toxic masculinity). He suffered through hot summer practices in the San Fernando Valley, at a time when adults would actually tell you that water was bad for you. When he reached his junior year of high school, his coach told him that he needed to keep his weight down to stay on the "B-team" (the equivalent of junior varsity). Since he wanted to play on the "A-team," he spent the summer packing on muscle, and thanks to an injury to someone else, he wound up as a starter.

In lieu of involved parents, Adam learned resilience and toughness from a fat guy huffing on a whistle.

He also learned about humility and teamwork. A two-way player (get your mind out of the gutter), Adam spent his offensive snaps on the line, clearing running lanes and protecting the quarterback. He took pride in doing a good job. The people in the stands might applaud the running back who jogs into the end zone, but Adam relished being one of the people who made that moment happen.

In his fourth year playing football, Adam dislocated his shoulder. (It actually stayed dislocated for three days before they could pop it back in with a sickening "clunk.") As you might expect, the injury ended his season. Even though Adam couldn't participate on the playing field with his teammates, he showed up faithfully to every game to support them. Sometimes actions speak louder than words.

Football's multitude of moving parts make it a great sport to teach teamwork, but it certainly isn't the only sport that does that. That's another important lesson learned from youth sports: your individual performance contributes to the success of a larger unit. Other people are depending on you, so you have to do your job. If an offensive lineman decides not to block, a running back can't score a touchdown. If a baserunner doesn't hustle around the bases, the batter might not get an RBI. (There is probably an equivalent example for lacrosse, but you'll have to Google it.)

Sports can give younger kids their first taste of accountability on top of adversity. When they mess up—because they *are* going to mess up—they can learn resiliency.

Not to sound too New Age here, but failures aren't failures if you can keep going and do better next time. The field of play is a great, low-consequence arena to hone the fine art of shrugging off the bad and looking forward to the next play.

Sports also instill a sense of poise and discipline.

Children, adorable little paradoxes that they are, both crave discipline and rebel against it. They'll push you to see how much they can get away with, but they need and want boundaries. Their mushy little minds don't realize it yet, but when you discipline them, it helps them understand that you care.

The challenge of parenting is balancing autonomy and discipline.

Mark grew up in Japan with his American parents and in that milieu was given a ton of independence at a very young age. He was literally taking the train back and forth to school in kindergarten—something that is unthinkable in America. As he grew older, Mark was given a lot of latitude. He had no curfew. There was essentially no micromanaging of his life, unless he screwed up. His Christian missionary mom's daily admonition was, "Remember whose you are and whom you serve."

Adam's parents... well, they figured out the autonomy part, so we'll give them partial credit. The need for structure (not provided by his parents) helped drive Adam to try out for Pop Warner football, and it was what kept him going back. He didn't understand it at the time, but his little seven-year-old heart and brain yearned for meaningful boundaries.

Dennis's parents figured out how to split the difference, giving him free reign of the city to build his independence, but insisting he attend the family's Shabbat dinner every Friday evening for some sense of structure.

This line isn't easy to walk. It's hard to know when to give your kids a little slack and when to rein them in.

But then again, no one ever said being a parent was easy. You have to do your best, allow yourself to mess up, and keep moving forward (the same skills you are trying to teach your kids). Someone is depending on you and watching every move you make.

Do you see now how these skills keep coming in handy?

$$\oslash$$

If you're a parent, there is one crucial thing you can do to help your child succeed in life: Keep your family intact.

We touched on this earlier, but truth deserves repetition: a child (of any race) who grows up with both of his parents in the household is in a better position than is a child (of any race) who grows up in a single parent household.

Statistics show that children who grow up in homes with both biological parents present tend to be better off financially. They're less likely to suffer from social and emotional issues; they're more likely to stay in school.

There are always outliers, of course. We hear about them often when we bring this point up during our campus appearances. During a question and answer session, someone will grab the microphone and eagerly tell us the story of some MacGregor P. MacTavish, who came from an orphanage and went on to found Nabisco. Bully for him! We aren't talking about outliers. We are talking about what works for the vast majority of people. (Put another way, one out of a thousand people who jump off the Golden Gate Bridge survives, but to be on the safe side, don't try it.)

Of course we aren't encouraging people to stay in relationships that are abusive or seriously dysfunctional. Sometimes you have to accept that life isn't going to be ideal. But in an ideal world, mom and dad are both decent people who stay together.

⊘

It is also important for parents to maintain and nurture relationships outside of their home. Put another way, it is important for parents to create a real-life "social network" beyond any online social networks.

Real-world connections and interactions are important. Children watch what we do and use us as role models, even if they don't always realize it. Like everyone (but probably at a more visceral level), children crave connection and derive joy from community. There are multiple ways to model healthy relationships with other people and organizations. This could look like inviting friends over for dinner or volunteering for charity organizations.

Being intentional about real-time relationships provides children with valuable social skills that are crucial later in life. Our culture is evolving to favor online interactions, and that's not necessarily a good change. We avoid talking to others as much as we can. Text messages have replaced phone calls. In the past, if we wanted a pizza delivered to our house, we called the pizza place and talked to someone. Now we order our pizza online, and it just shows up. Barroom arguments that previously would have ended up with each party buying the other a beer (even if it took some fisticuffs along the way) have now given way to bitter Twitter arguments that almost never have a happy ending. How is this a better way to live—not to mention, to produce productive members of society? How is insulating yourself from real-life situations going to teach your children how to cope as they grow up?

This critique, by the way, comes from someone who is trying to educate America with five-minute online videos. Dennis Prager is definitely not telling you to unplug the computer, cast out your electronics, churn your own butter, raise a barn, and get crazy Amish. (Even if he believed it, it would cost Dennis too much money.)

Yet human interaction civilizes us. We're less likely to insult people to their faces. If what someone says insults us, we are much more likely to talk it through in person. Hiding behind a keyboard offers the illusion of safety and silences our internal gatekeepers. We feel like we have permission to spout off, and immunity from the consequences.

We need to lift our eyes up off our phones and pay attention to the world we live in. How else can we can demand our kids do the same? You have to walk the walk to talk the talk.

A benefit to actively participating in the world around you is that it introduces you to your community and helps you forge bonds with your neighbors. It doesn't mean you have to be the life of every block party. What it does mean is that you need to cultivate parenting allies. If you're trying to let your kids have some autonomy, it helps to have extra sets of eyes in your community. You want your neighbors to feel comfortable yelling at (or using the dad or mom voice with) your kids, if your kids have it coming. You also want your kids to have a healthy amount of respect for adults. That way, when your neighbor threatens your child with a well-placed phone call (or a wooden spoon or a flip-flop to their behind), it permeates their mushy little minds and reminds them to straighten up and fly right. Or else.

⊘

Adam Carolla's strong sense of determination is a big part of why Dennis decided to embark on the *No Safe Spaces* tour with him. It's something the two of them share.

They had very different upbringings. Adam didn't have many deep father-son conversations with his dad, but there was one piece of advice that stood out to him. As you might expect, it was totally accidental: he told young Adam, "Whatever happens, it will be your fault."

That turned out to be great (almost prophetic) advice. It encouraged Adam to develop self-reliance and personal responsibility. Of course there are exceptions to what you can control; you could always get hit by a bus, or come down with Ebola, or get swept up by a tornado and launched into a mountain. Yet there is so much we can do to direct our own fates that the exceptions aren't worth wringing our hands over. If you can instill in your children the idea that everything that happens within their own control—good or bad—is their own fault and the result of their own efforts, you will have given them a head start on most of their peers when it comes to life skills.

⊘

Every so often, Dennis will take a call on his radio show from a concerned parent. The conversation will go something like this:

Dennis, the worried mom will say, I have a daughter at [insert name of college]. Politically, she leans conservative. But she knows that if she shares her own opinion when a professor asks her to write a paper, her grade will suffer. If she parrots the professor's talking points, with which she doesn't agree, she will get a better grade.

"What should I tell her to do?"

Many students face this situation in school; it puts parents in a tough spot and leaves them feeling conflicted.

As you might expect, we have strong opinions on this subject (and you probably already know what they are). Instead of our telling you what we would do in that situation, here's a question to ask yourself (and then ask your daughter).

If you compromise on this point, where do you draw the line?

If you're willing to compromise your beliefs here, where else will you be willing to compromise your beliefs and values? When you're filling out tax returns? At work? In your marriage?

If you're willing to be untruthful about your views to get a better test grade, then there are clearly situations in which you consider it acceptable to be untruthful. So where do you draw the line?

Part of being a parent means helping your son or daughter draw that line. It is important to raise kids who are mentally and emotionally solid, but they'll still need your love and support if and when they refuse to sell out for a summa cum laude.

EXTRA CREDIT: JORDAN PETERSON ON PREPARING STUDENTS FOR A HAPPY LIFE

Jordan Peterson has lectured extensively on how to forge a fulfilling life, and he spoke on the topic when he visited Adam's garage. He offered some good ideas for parents to keep in mind:

What you need to provide students with is an identity. For me, an identity is a set of tools to operate with in the world. You want your child to go to university and to pick up a set of tools that they can use to operate within the world and be successful, to be successful at the things that people do when they're successful. Finding a partner, establishing a network of friends, picking a career, you know, acting forthrightly in the world.

All of these things that make for a noble individual existence. If you tell them instead that the game is rigged, especially against people like you, and the people who are rigging it will never let go of their power, and the only reason they have it is because it's power and tyranny, not ability and sacrifice, then, well, how could you not emerge from that broken and depressed? And I've had many, many people write to me, and you can see this in the comments on my YouTube channel, detailing their experiences once they leap out of the cult and noting that it's taken them years to recover from that world view.

It's so pathological. And it's also untrue. Like, you could easily tell students, look, one of the factors that might contribute to people's success is that they have membership in the dominant ethnical racial gender group. I think you can say that all things considered, in any society, if you're a member of the majority, things are easier for you. But the question is to what degree does that make a difference? And the answer is, in our societies, it makes some difference.

But it isn't the determining factor. There's no evidence that it's the determining factor. Lots of people who are immigrants and the children of first-generation immigrants do spectacularly well....

Say there [are] things that determine whether or not you're successful and having a majority racial profile would be one of them. And maybe it would be ranked seventeenth out of twenty. Now, I don't know what it is exactly, but you could say that credibly.... Most people overcome at least one major obstacle. You're very, very hard-pressed to find someone who isn't seriously disadvantaged in at least one dimension.

⊘

I know lots of wealthy people, and first of all, the psychological data on wealth is quite clear. It [shows that] once you have enough money that the bill collectors aren't chasing you around, additional money makes absolutely no difference to your psychological wellbeing. It can remove misery, but it can't add happiness. And part of the reason for that is that if you're well-placed socioeconomically, well, your family members still get old. You're likely to have someone who's near and dear to you who's suffering from some terrible illness of some sort or who is likely to within the next ten years. You're hardly immune from divorce. You have the same family struggles as everyone else. They're not exaggerated by poverty, but also very few people are in the position where abject poverty is the problem....

That's also an argument against materialism as a fundamental philosophy. It is the case that money can actually solve a fairly narrow range of life's problems. And some of them, it exacerbates. So, you know, if you're impulsive and poorly controlled, the last thing you need is money. It'll just wipe you out.

There is an old psychoanalytic idea that I really liked, and I think it was developed initially by Freud, that the good mother necessarily fails. If you're a good mother, you have an infant, you take care of the infant's every desire, especially, say, a six-month-old child or younger than that. The infant is always right, right? If the infant cries, you bloody well do something. You don't argue with an infant....

But that doesn't work once the kid starts to hit even nine months or certainly not by two because the child starts to develop some autonomy. And then that autonomy grows—and the mother has to pull back and "fail," let's say, as the child becomes more and more autonomous.

One idea is that you protect people by protecting, and the other is you embolden them by encouraging them. That's a whole different thing, and it's the right thing, right, because you can't protect people. Life's a fatal disease, right? That's the old joke: it's a sexually transmissible disease that's 100% fatal. You're not going to protect people from that. And so the best you can do is to make them strong.

I always tell my students the opposite: You're so tough and mean, you can't even bloody well fathom it. And if you were put in a situation where it was necessary that you manifest that, you would learn that very quickly. You're a monster, and that's actually a good thing because the world, life is monstrous, and unless you have the monstrosity to prevail under those circumstances, you're going to get rolled over. Now, you should be a civilized monster, right? That's the right thing to aim at. But to tell people, "No, the world is a terribly scary place, and you're so weak that you need to be fenced in constantly," .... well, it's the castrating mother from the Freudian nightmare.

$\oslash$

I did a series of Biblical lectures. I have twelve of them now. And I took apart the story of Cain and Abel. And Cain and Abel is a very instructive story, even though it's only a paragraph long.[1]

Abel and Cain both make sacrifices—they burn animals, right? They actually act out the process of sacrifice. But it has the same psychological meaning. People make sacrifices to get ahead. Sometimes, your sacrifices are rewarded, and sometimes, they're not. And maybe that's because God's just in a bad mood and has decided not to smile on you, or maybe it's because there's something wrong with your damn sacrifice. You're just not trying hard enough. Well, anyways, Cain's sacrifices are rejected. So he goes and has a little chat with God, and he says, look, I'm breaking myself in half here trying to put my life together, and everything's going well for Abel, and nothing's going well for me. What sort of stupid universe did you make, anyways?

And God basically says... "Don't be criticizing the structure of the universe before you put your own house in order." That's the last thing Cain wants to hear. So when Cain leaves his little discussion with God, the story says his countenance falls which means that he becomes resentful and enraged. And the first thing he does is kill Abel.

That's the first story about human beings in the Bible. Because Adam and Eve were made by God. They're not real people, right? So, the first two human beings engage in exactly what we're seeing being acted out politically.

CHAPTER FOURTEEN

HOW EDUCATORS CAN DO BETTER

A nyone who has had kids knows that sometimes your voice isn't the most persuasive. Peers, coaches, and teachers all play a part in your child's development.

No matter how many curfews you set or instructions you give about staying out of trouble, a friend (especially a boyfriend or girl-friend) makes a compelling counter-argument. After-school specials call it "peer pressure."

Having other adults scolding your kids actually can be helpful if the other voices are singing to your child from the same sheet of music. After you instill autonomy and discipline in your kids, having those messages echoed by their academic institutions, friends' parents, coaches, and other authoritative voices will help reinforce the lessons.

But as we have seen, problems created by bad parenting can be made worse when professors and faculty refuse to rein in students' impulses. Overprotective parents are sending little narcissists off to school, and the schools certainly aren't doing anything to correct their self-important tendencies. And that ruins everyone's fun.

Even before students arrive at college, educators have been reinforcing the wrong message. After all, students spend four years in high school. If we're going to solve the problems in higher education, we're going to have to look at the education system as a whole.

$$\oslash$$

While they don't have as much autonomy as they will have in college, high school students have more independence than they had in elementary or middle school.

In high school, students start to have a hand in building their own academic schedules. Rather than having grade-level subjects across the board, students may be distributed across different academic tiers depending on their aptitude and interest. They choose elective courses in addition to their general education requirements. They have more extracurricular activities—sports, clubs, and nonsports competition groups such as math or debate teams. They organize events and fundraisers with some limited adult guidance and supervision, instead of having their activities dictated to them like their younger counterparts.

This seems like a good place to start.

To churn out better graduates, every public high school in America should immediately implement the following six changes.

1. Schools should immediately cease to honor race or ethnicity. Regardless of whether students are black, brown, red, yellow, or white; regardless of whether their origins are Africa, Europe, Latin America or Asia; regardless of whether their ancestors showed up on the Mayflower or on a slave ship, the only identity a school should recognize is each student's unique and individual identity. Every student should be judged solely on his or her own character, scholarship, and humanity. The only national identity a school ought to recognize is American. (After all, American public schools should be in the business of helping to create better Americans, right?)

Incidentally, this change should extend to extracurricular activities. No principal should promote clubs that divide students based on race, ethnicity, sexual orientation, or whatever other characteristic becomes en vogue. Clubs like these promote narcissism; if you join a club based on your own demographics, what you are really saying is that little interests you outside of your own self. Since the purpose of education is to get you to think beyond yourself, school clubs and activities should instead be based on common interests and passions— clubs that transport you to the wonders and glories of art, music, astronomy, languages you don't already speak, and more.

2. Prioritize the English language. Every student should leave high school speaking and writing English as fluently as possible. Any school that doesn't ensure students leave with excellent English language skills is remiss in its duty to prepare graduates for the job market.

This is not a nativist position—schools should teach other languages. (It is deplorable that so many Americans can only speak one language.) However, teaching non-language classes in a foreign language does no one any favors. Quite the contrary: it severely limits those students' options after high school.

3. Everything in a school should reflect the fact that learning is a sacred endeavor. The process deserves respect. For that reason, schools should have dress codes to ensure that students (and teachers) wear appropriate attire for the undertaking. And students should address teachers respectfully using their title and last name: "Mrs. Jones," "Ms. Smith," "Miss Ramirez," or "Mr. Martinez," for example. First names are a non-starter; we're talking about teachers, not pals.

4. No obscene language. This principle may sound strange in a book that champions the concept of free expression. But foul language is disrespectful and distracts from a school's educational mission, and it blurs the distinction between the elevated and the degraded. Obscenity shouldn't be tolerated anywhere on school grounds. This would include the words you can't say on television, and it would also include the word "bitch" (even if used when one girl addresses another) and the n-word (even if used when one black student addresses another).

5. End all programs that superficially build self-esteem. Despite what their promoters would have you believe, self-esteem can truly be achieved in only one way: it must be earned. Programs that seek to instill self-esteem in any other way are trafficking in falsehoods. And schools should have one valedictorian, not seven.

6. Every school should be re-oriented toward academics and away from politics. Schools should stop expending efforts on issues like racism, sexism, Islamophobia, homophobia, global warming, tobacco, and gender identity; they should devote no more classes that teach students how to wear condoms and treat sexual relations as nothing

more than a health issue. Most importantly, there should be no more attempts to convince anyone that he or she is a victim because he or she is not white, male, heterosexual, or Christian. (Conversely, students should not be told they have an unfair advantage because they are white, male, heterosexual, or Christian, either.)

If high schools are doing their jobs, graduates will leave feeling inordinately lucky: lucky to be alive and lucky to be Americans. (As we'll discuss later, that's probably the limit of how lucky we want them to feel.)

They will also have a sound understanding of and appreciation for the educational environment. When they show up in a classroom, whether it's in their high school or on a college campus, they should expect a rigorous search for truth above all else, rather than the false values of comfort, tolerance, and universal acceptance.

This would challenge colleges and universities to rise to those expectations and support the search for truth, as their mission dictates.

$\oslash$

Oklahoma Wesleyan University is half a continent away from the University of California at Berkeley. Ideologically, it's much further away.

But even this overtly conservative, Christian institution thirty-five miles outside of Tulsa, Oklahoma, couldn't escape calls for trigger warnings. In fact, back in November 2015, a student raised concerns after a pre-Thanksgiving chapel homily on 1 Corinthians 13. If you're not familiar with that part of the Bible (Adam was, but Dennis had to look it up), it's a section you likely have heard if you've ever been to a wedding in a church. It's about love, and it's a relatively innocuous passage at that. It gets read at weddings because it says things like "love is patient, love is kind"—thus ranking it as among the least-likely verses to prompt drunken fisticuffs between newly minted relatives at the reception.

Still, someone at this conservative Christian school who for some reason felt "singled out" managed to be offended.

Dr. Everett Piper, President of Oklahoma Wesleyan, couldn't believe it. The situation moved him to write a blog post entitled "This Is Not a Daycare, It's a University!"—and eventually an entire book titled *Not a Daycare: The Devastating Consequences of Abandoning Truth*.[1]

Without revealing the student's name, Piper admonished him and others that sermons and homilies are supposed to make listeners feel uncomfortable—and even guilty. "If you want the chaplain to tell you you're a victim rather than tell you that you need virtue," Piper wrote, "this may not be the university you're looking for."

In 2017, Piper visited Dennis's radio show and Adam's podcast on the same day. He expressed worry that institutions of higher education are abandoning the pursuit of truth in favor of superficial tolerance.

Many view political correctness as an affront to free speech. Piper took it a step further, noting the concepts espoused by politically correct culture don't make sense—and if your job is education, shouldn't your words make sense? "Stop and think about the way we've raised our current generation of kids and leaders," Piper said. "We've actually taught them that it makes sense to say, 'I can't tolerate your intolerance,' or 'I hate you hateful people.'"

"My industry, higher education, is guilty of peddling this pablum to the next generation of leaders."

In abandoning the search for truth and embracing moral relativism, colleges are really turning their backs on education. If there is no truth to discover—if there is nothing definite to learn—how can you get smarter?

Piper recalled an example from a freshman orientation seminar he gave at a different college. He wanted to get students thinking about the consequences of ideas, so he assigned them the movie *Schindler's List*. Each student was to write a five-page paper describing how someone like Adolph Hitler could come to power. One young lady's paper included a very good summary of the film, but it ended by asking the question, "Who am I to judge the Germans?"

You know moral relativism is off the rails when someone twists herself into such mental knots that she can't even call Nazis bad.

Faculty need to prioritize learning over comfort. Essential to that process is abandoning easy answers. Part of the appeal of identity politics is the easiness of the answer. But while telling students that any shortcomings in their lives are the result of bias or someone else's privilege may be an easy sell in the short term, it does not help them—and may actually harm them.

Pointing to the wealthiest people with a shrug and saying they got where they are because of unfair inherent advantages cheats students out of learning what it takes to be successful. Most wealthy, successful people got where they are with hard work, opportunism, determination, and grit. Disguising that fact by pointing to the rare examples of trust-fund babies who never work a day and imagining that's the norm sets graduates up to fail when they enter the work force.

Finally, educators can't be afraid to establish discipline and rigorous academic standards, letting students succeed based on their own merits.

Piper shared a metaphor from the Catholic author and philosopher G. K. Chesterton. Chesterton said that if you built the greatest, most fun playground in the world, you would still need a fence. There were two reasons: first, children need boundaries (without the fence, they would run out into the street, Chesterton reasoned); second, without the fence, adults would constantly be herding children into the center.

If you think about it, Chesterton was right. Paradoxically, clear limits create freedom. If there's not a fence, an adult has to create a restriction every time a child strays too far in one direction. So teachers and parents erect imaginary mental fences—and since those are super easy to get through, they have to keep putting up more. The result is parents and educators constantly saying, "No," and kids who are miserable. In contrast, putting one actual fence up to mark the boundary eliminates the need for all of those smaller mental fences.

The same is true on campus. Setting very broadly defined boundaries for discussion and debate and then letting people figure things out within those boundaries is much preferable to a hodgepodge of ad hoc, situational restrictions.

Of course, professors need to be able to look to others—students and colleagues are good places to start—to check their own tendencies to create classroom experiences that are biased toward politics, to the neglect of the search for truth.

Students may be children when they enter the campus gates, but they should be adults by the time they leave—and that will only happen if faculty and administrators eschew coddling them and instead challenge them.

⊘

You can see the promise of higher education in the collaboration—and friendship—between Professors Cornel West and Robert George.

The Ivy League veterans don't initially jump out at you as two fellows who would obviously work together. George, a Roman Catholic and political conservative, teaches constitutional law at Princeton. With his placid smile, gray hair, and wire-framed glasses, he looks like he might be at home in a college classroom. West has created hip-hop CDs and written bestselling books on racial politics. The streaks of gray in his high afro and beard testify to more than three decades as a leading voice in left-wing philosophy.

In today's political environment, you might expect any "collaboration" between two people with these credentials to involve insults, cable news bickering, and maybe one of them trying to hit the other with a metal folding chair. Yet West and George have been teaching courses together since 2007, and not a single lecture has ended in fisticuffs.

When Dennis and Adam sat down to interview them for the *No Safe Spaces* movie, George explained that he and West are able to engage one another respectfully because both professors recognize the value of hearing each other out.

"We're a pair of old-fashioned humanists," George told us. "We believe in the power of ideas, the importance of exposing our students to the best that has been thought and said on both sides—or all sides—of the important questions of meaning and value."

Being open to ideas and allowing people to investigate and question them is what George and West assert higher education should be all about. They envision classrooms that foster what West called, "a fundamental commitment to a robust and uninhibited Socratic dialogue, in which people can enter the public space without humiliation, and have their views mediated with a certain respect—but also serious intellectual interrogation."

Yet as George and West saw their own partnership flourishing, they noticed their mutual respect becoming more and more of an outlier among fellow academics. Controversial views—those that didn't adhere to the dominant philosophies—were getting shouted down and shut out of classrooms. Guest speakers who brought differing views were being dis-invited from campuses. (See? We told you we weren't the first ones.)

According to West, none of this is new.

"There's a long history in this country of universities having dogmatic forms of censorship," he explained. For much of the twentieth century, that censorship was directed at West's own ideological brethren: in the 1920s, colleges targeted pacifists who opposed the United States jumping into World War I, and the 1950s saw Senator Joseph McCarthy's zealous anti-communism replicated on many campuses.

West doesn't want to see a repeat of such censorship, regardless of who the target is.

"We have to be suspicious of all forms of hegemony, all forms of dogmatism in universities across the board," West warned.

"The pursuit of truth," added George, "cannot flourish in the absence of freedom of thought and expression."

West and George have been working to convince colleges to return to that kind of open forum. In 2017, they released a joint statement about modern academia entitled "Truth Seeking, Democracy and Freedom of Thought and Expression:"[2]

> The pursuit of knowledge and the maintenance of a free and democratic society require the cultivation and practice of the virtues of intellectual humility, openness of mind, and, above all, love of truth. These virtues will manifest themselves and be strengthened by one's willingness to listen attentively and respectfully to intelligent people who challenge one's beliefs and who represent causes one disagrees with and points of view one does not share.
>
> That's why all of us should seek respectfully to engage with people who challenge our views. And we should oppose efforts to silence those with whom we disagree—especially on college and university campuses.

And that's just the beginning. Their statement goes on to encourage people to do things like "listen" and "respectfully engage those with whom we disagree"—things that should be laughably obvious. It could very well be a mission statement for higher education writ large, which is why it already boasts hundreds of co-signers from all walks of life and several dozen from the ranks of academia.

The fact is, areas of discomfort, friction, disagreement, and danger are best dealt with head on. Efforts to tamp down free thought in the name of comfort may seem like protection, but really are just dereliction of duty.

⊘

West worries about what we all—and not just those in academia—lose when we sacrifice free thought and free expression. He fears that the breakdown of academic freedom and expression on campus has dire consequences for the future of America as a nation, as institutions of higher learning churn out an assembly line of graduates who have spent four years having their worldview delicately handled with kid gloves.

"When you try to create a safe space in which it's difficult to be unsettled, unnerved, [and] challenged, you reinforce silos," warns West, "you reinforce bubbles. You reinforce walls, which makes it difficult for you to cultivate the capacity to learn from other people."

"Especially," West adds, "people you disagree with."

West cites John Dewey, the nineteenth-century philosopher and psychologist, "John Dewey said, show me a democracy in which people deride and denounce and devalue public conversations, I'll show you a democracy that's unravelling and on its way to authoritarian rule."

"And John Dewey's right about that."

EXTRA CREDIT: EVERETT PIPER ON TEACHING VIRTUE

Everett Piper, president of Oklahoma Wesleyan University, had more to say about the importance of teaching virtue:

When you stop teaching virtue and you start teaching victimization, you shouldn't be surprised at the eventual and violent culture and reaction. In other words, there's no basis for any cultural engagement, any community involvement that's virtuous any longer because we laugh at virtue.

In fact, I think C.S. Lewis says in *The Abolition of Man* that we laugh at honor and are shocked to find traitors in our midst. We sever the organ and demand the function. We geld the stallion and bid him be fruitful. Well, when we have cut out the organ, the organ of virtue, the heart, the soul, the character of the human being, when we dumb down the *Imago Dei* to the *Imago Dog*, then we shouldn't be surprised to see people acting like animals because they haven't been taught that they're any different than that....

We elevate the human being to the highest definition through this process of higher education. And that elevation of human identity is the *Imago Dei*, the image of God. That gives us the ability to argue and debate and to disagree and to come to conclusions. It gives us the ability to pursue what's true. It gives us the ability and the responsibility to be a virtuous people because we understand virtue. So education should be targeted at that ultimate goal. Not just the acquisition of information. Education should be about ethics, not information. It should be about morality, not just money. It should be about character, not just how to acquire a better job, a career....

A liberal arts institution was established let's say 1,000 years ago at Oxford. To do what? To educate a free man, a free woman, a free people, a free culture, a free society— an education in freedom and liberty and liberation. That's what a liberal arts education was supposed to be for. And today we've lost the context of that.... Oxford to this day has one word on its shield: "*Veritas*," Latin for truth. Northwestern University has Philippians, Paul's letter to the Philippians, as its motto. "Whatever is true." And they don't even know it any longer. Berkeley's motto is: "Let there be Light," a reference to Genesis....

Berkeley isn't the birthplace of free speech; I would argue that Bethlehem is, because it's in the words of Christ that we hear, "You shall know the truth and the truth shall set you free." And it's in the protests at Berkeley that you see ideological fascism as opposed to academic freedom prevailing today.

$$\oslash$$

I've been asked a thousand times how we got into this mess. And I would argue it's my industry's fault. It's higher education's fault. It's the ivory tower's fault. We created this monster, and it's turning around to consume us right now. And how did we create it? Well, we've been teaching lousy ideas, decade after decade after decade. As I've said, Richard Weaver wrote a seminal work in 1948, and he titled it *Ideas Have Consequences*. And his point was simple: ideas have consequences. They always lead somewhere. Good ideas lead to good culture, good kids, and good community. And bad ideas lead to the opposite. Like your grandmother said, garbage in and garbage out. So higher education has been teaching self-absorption and narcissism for some thirty, forty, fifty years, and now all of a sudden we're surprised? We're surprised to find a self-absorbed and narcissistic populace? We're surprised to see students acting selfishly on the campus green and in the classroom?

We taught them to behave that way. We taught them that it doesn't matter what you believe as long as it works for you. We have been pedaling this pablum of value neutrality for decades, and now we're shocked that they have no values and they have no virtue? Of course they're going to think this way because we told them to. Higher education is responsible. The university is at fault.

⊘

One of the things that I've been asked about my original op-ed ("This Is Not a Daycare. It's a University!") and the subsequent book is, why is it happening, and where are the rest of your peers? Where are the faculty, and where are the college presidents saying the same thing? Well frankly, I think it's because there are so few of us out there with any spine, any courage. I think people are more interested in protecting their careers and protecting their positions than they are in dealing with the problem. They're afraid. And I think that fear has resulted in them just sitting on their hands and remaining silent. I've had numerous people come up to me and say, I agree with you, but I can't speak publicly. You know another interesting thing is those that do agree with me and have said so.

$$\oslash$$

Is this a problem just for the state university? Absolutely not…. I think the Christian colleges are, in many cases, sadly as guilty of losing their way as the secular academy. I did my dissertation on this at Michigan State University. I wanted to understand what the constituents of Christian colleges believe the words "evangelical Christian" or "liberal arts" mean when they attend an institution and they pay for it. And I found that the Christian University lacks clarity and mission just as much, if not more so, than the secular university. I had faculty tell me that the stories of Jesus's death, his resurrection, his virgin birth, and his miracles didn't have to be "reality statements," they could be "message statements." I had a board member tell me that she had searched the Scriptures over and over again and could find nothing in them that said that premarital or extra-marital sexual relationships were unhealthy.

And this is at a Christian institution that is supposed to be boldly and unapologetically Christ-centered, Biblically-driven, and grounded in a Judeo-Christian ethics. But if we can't clarify even to ourselves that the stories of Jesus are true as opposed to myth, and that the moral directives in Scriptures are clear, then I would argue that we're not giving our students a very good product at the end of the day, because we don't even know what it is that we want to teach them.

CHAPTER FIFTEEN

GET HAPPY (OR, THIS IS ALL YOUR RESPONSIBILITY)

I magine you're stopped at a red light when some yahoo behind you who is frantically tweeting about something lets his foot off the brake. You're waiting for the light to change when he rolls into you. You hear the crunch, then you feel it. You lurch forward a little before Skippy McTweetstorm realizes what he's done and slams on his brakes.

But it's too late. You've been rear-ended.

It's not your fault, but getting your car fixed—talking to your insurance company, getting the quote, finding a repair shop, making an appointment, and all of that—has become your responsibility. The damage won't get fixed on its own. Assuming that the other guy is insured, the work will be paid for, but there's still time being sucked out of your life as you deal with the aftermath of this little accident.

Anyone who has been in a fender bender like this knows the difference between fault and responsibility.

The current environment on campus is the product of decades upon decades of administrators and faculty doing their best to close their own minds and the minds of their students. Today's students are not to blame for the problem. Adults who knew better should have stepped in and prevented things from getting this bad.

But if you're a student (or even a former student), it's up to you to get your mind right and succeed—despite what you've been taught. You are responsible for your own success.

Trust us. You wouldn't want it any other way.

$$\oslash$$

Adam likes to remind people that he's not lucky.

Yes, that's the same guy who lives in a big house, has a great career, and owns Paul Newman's race car. But that embarrassment of riches didn't happen by luck. You have heard about his upbringing—from the poverty to the uninterested parents to the 1.7 GPA at North Hollywood (buoyed by six A's he got by playing football). You remember that his diploma qualified him to dig ditches and clean carpets. Or at least it would have qualified him for those jobs, had he had ever received it. Thanks to the small matter of an unreturned textbook, North Hollywood High didn't give Adam a diploma—not that any job he took in those early years would have asked for it.

("Look, we think you would do a boffo job picking up garbage, but we really need to know that you mastered algebra.")

While Adam's buddies went out and had fun after work, he took classes at the Improv, learning how to perform onstage. And he didn't go there on scholarship; Adam scraped the money together to pay for those classes. Unfortunately, they don't give Pell grants for improv classes. Then he spent his free time trying to get onstage at open mic nights.

His "big break" came when he met Jimmy Kimmel and cracked into radio at KROQ. But he didn't bump into Kimmel at a convenience store. Kimmel didn't catch him at an open mic night and then go urge his bosses to put him on the air. Adam went down to the radio station. He found Kimmel. He used his experience as a boxing trainer (a side hustle he had picked up) and created an opportunity to train Kimmel for a promotional boxing match.

Adam's a funny guy, but there are a lot of funny guys out there. He's not lucky. He's notorious among his friends for losing Super Bowl bets. If he had relied on his luck, you would probably find him wasting away on a futon in a one-bedroom North Hollywood apartment today scratching off lottery tickets.

Lottery tickets, by the way, are a scam. You aren't going to win the lottery. You also don't have a long-lost rich uncle who's going to leave you $1 billion when he kicks the bucket. You're lucky to be alive and relatively healthy. That is about the only good luck you can hope for.

Think of it this way: if your resume is sitting on a desk side-by-side with someone else's resume, and the two are so equal that a hiring manager uses the flip of a coin to decide whom to hire, assume you will lose that flip every single time.

What is the solution? Don't let your resume be equal to other people's. Make it better. Refuse to settle for mediocrity and instead strive for excellence.

You earn your luck with your own actions, just like Adam did.

"Earn" is an apt verb to use here. It is one of the most beautiful words in the English language. In Spanish, French, and other romantic languages, the verb "to earn" is the same as the verb "to win." But earning success isn't the same as winning a game of chance. Earning means putting in the work and creating the desired result. It means you choose your own direction.

It means responsibility—but also the freedom and empowerment that come only with responsibility.

For example, you get to choose what irritates you.

Did someone say something politically incorrect on Twitter? You can decide to let that upset you, ruin your day, and eat up hours of your life as you get the offending person kicked off social media and end up in a big Internet fight with his friends and supporters. Or you can mutter "Idiot" under your breath and get on with your life.

The latter attitude would instantly eliminate the controversies many colleges and cities are dealing with over old Confederate statues. But instead people protest and demonstrate, demanding a statue be torn down. But statues can't hurt people, or attack them. As a matter of fact, they don't move. Outside of horror movies, if you walk past a statue, it doesn't follow you. And buildings, even buildings named after slave owners such as George Washington and Thomas Jefferson, can't hurt you either—short of a chunk of loose masonry falling on your head. So who cares what someone names a building?

If passive objects bother you, it's because you let them bother you—and that's on you. It is not your fault some racist back in the 1930s paid for a statue of Stonewall Jackson because he wanted to intimidate black people. But it's your responsibility to keep it from affecting the things you want to do to be successful.

By taking responsibility for your own state of mind, you abandon the idea of victimhood, the concept that other people are capable of holding you back and that society is fixed to prevent you from succeeding.

The victimhood mentality is completely incompatible with the sense of responsibility that creates success. It's a handicap, but unlike a physical or mental disability, it's avoidable. We've spent chapters talking about its ill effects, and we've encouraged parents and teachers not to instill it in students. But the victimhood mentality is like black mold in the basement of a house—once even a little bit takes hold, it starts to spread and eat away at the structures. And there is only one person who can really protect you from its deleterious effects: you.

If you want to see the effects of this mentality, look at daytime television. When children of the 1970s and 1980s faked an illness to stay home watching syndicated reruns of *Good Times*, they might have seen commercials for Wally Thorpe's School of Long Haul Trucking or Sally Struthers peddling a correspondence course to learn VCR repair. These commercials were aimed at people watching television at noon on a Tuesday: people who were out of work, but who wanted to work. If you were out of work and wanted to get to work, you might want to learn how to drive an eighteen-wheeler.

Today's daytime TV commercials are very different. They may start with a line like, "Were you wrongfully let go?" or, "Were you hurt in an automobile accident?" Cut to a stern looking guy in a suit claiming to be the lawyer who will fight to get you the money you deserve. We've gone from appealing to people's desire to build a better life for themselves to catering to the fantasy of an unearned payout.

The tragedy here is that we can all change with the right mindset. (And, if we're being honest, most of the people in your life want you to change, in one way or another. Even your parents can tell you that you're the most perfect thing they every created, but they probably wish you'd call more often.) The idea that something good will happen to you without any effort on your part—whether it's a lucky lottery ticket or a big legal settlement because a bus door closed on your finger—invites you to remain who you are. The simple truth is that if you want to change your situation in life, you have to change yourself.

Too often we look to authority figures, especially politicians, to solve our problems for us. And politicians, who tend to fall less on the side of "stand-up folks telling hard truths" and more on the side of "high-functioning narcissists looking to win their next election however they can," are more than happy to indulge us. They will hold rallies or town hall meetings, point to you in the audience, and promise that, if elected, "I'll fight for you!"

What a ridiculous thing to say. First, that politician doesn't know you. Second, you know he's going to go to the next campaign event one town over, look at another crowd, and promise some other poor sap, "I'll fight for you!" Is that politician going to fight for *everyone?* He'll be busy, and if it gets to actual fighting, there would probably be some charges filed.

Ask yourself this: is that politician just saying what he thinks you want to hear? It may sound crazy, but stick with us here. Politicians might just possibly be lying to the voters.

And they get away with it because of the voters' expectations. Every four years during the presidential primaries, some cable news channel shows a town hall meeting with the candidates. A woman stands up and tell some sob story about being pregnant with triplets and on academic probation at the community college. Then she asks, "What are you going to do for me?"

No matter what the candidate actually says, the honest-to-goodness answer is: "Nothing."

The politicians can prattle on about this government program or that one, but the only real chance this woman has of achieving a better life comes from her own ability and determination. Even if the government did try to institute a program to help her out, we all know they would screw it up, right? These people can't figure out how to deliver mail or fix roads, but everyone is sure they can fix all our problems: *Sure, that bridge they built collapsed and killed a bunch of people, but maybe let's put them in charge of running healthcare and lifting people out of poverty.*

Another phrase politicians like to throw out there is "creating a level playing field." There's no such thing. (In fact, real playing fields are not level. The nicest football fields tend to be crowned in the middle for drainage.) The reality is that people have different challenges. Some people are faster than others. Some are smarter. Some people are short, or fat, or have one arm smaller than the other. Government can't do anything about all of that. Governments can fight wars. And they might be able to stop a plague. But you are responsible for yourself and your family. The best you can hope for is not a perfectly level playing field but a clear one, without any unnatural obstructions like landmines or barbed wire, so you have a chance to make it through on your own devices.

When someone asks for your vote by saying, "I'll fight for you," or, "I'll level the playing field," or otherwise promises to get rid of all your problems, that's a good indication that the candidate doesn't deserve your vote.

The promise to do things for people has led to the rise of a "language of losers," which expresses the way too many Americans—especially students and recent graduates—view their lives.

Using the language of losers is the opposite of taking responsibility and initiative. It means finding excuses. If you want to succeed in the workplace, you need to cut the loser language out of your vocabulary right now.

We have seen this when working with younger employees, softened by the educational system from kindergarten through college. When they mess up, some will defend themselves by saying, "I did my best."

We tell kids this all the time, "Do your best, little Johnny." It starts as an encouragement: "Hey, maybe you can't write *The Iliad* yet, but it's first grade. Don't be afraid of a few misspellings. Failure is just a chance to learn. So do your best, and we'll work on what needs to get better." But somehow this encouragement for children has morphed into an endgame for adults.

If an employee screws up and tells us, "I did my best," we fire that employee. The right answer is, "I screwed up, and I'll do better next time" (or "I'm drunk, and I need to sit down").

It isn't enough to do *your* best; you need to do *the* best.

Younger employees also tend to tell you how they feel. Here is a super-special secret, so listen closely: No one gives a crap about your feelings. You're twenty-three, living with your parents, sleeping in a bed shaped like a race car, and your professional accomplishments so far involve getting to work without being hit by a cattle truck. Congratulations. You have accomplished exactly nothing yet. Do something significant, and then someone might care about how you feel.

In professional environments, you need to work hard and dedicate yourself to producing excellent work. If you do that, you will be rewarded. Either your employer will reward you, or someone else will find you, hire you, and reward you. Internalizing responsibility for yourself gives you that opportunity.

$$\oslash$$

All this sounds like an oversized helping of tough love, which is an odd way to spend the first chunk of a chapter on happiness.

But as you can tell, neither of us is a big proponent of self-esteem the way it is generally understood. Self-esteem programs in public schools drive home the mantra that everyone is unique and special in his or her own way—a delicate snowflake unlike any other in the word. The underlying theme is that each person's value is inherent in his or her uniqueness.

While it's important to recognize human dignity—it's really helpful in interpersonal relationships, assuming you aren't a serial killer—simple existence does not make anyone excellent. What these programs breed is a sense of entitlement. And entitlement is the polar opposite of gratitude, which, more than any other human trait, leads to happiness.

Ingratitude creates anger. It gives you permission to feel like a victim. It makes you resent others. And if you resent others, and you're angry and jealous, you lash out emotionally, verbally, and physically. Ingratitude makes you a miserable and harmful person.

Gratitude, on the other hand, comes from the belief that everything you (or anyone else) has is earned—and that you are entitled to none of it. The less you feel entitled to, the more gratitude you will have and the happier you will be.

Do not confuse gratitude and feeling unentitled with a lack of desire or ambition.

Say you have a friend with a big three-story house with a big yard, beautiful landscaping, and the kind of porch you could spend the whole day sitting on in a rocking chair drinking lemonade. Meanwhile you live in a small, single-floor ranch house with a brown lawn and a rusty storm door. You can think of this in one of two ways.

You might go down the path of envy and entitlement. "I work really hard digging ditches," you might think. "My neighbor sits in an air-conditioned office, doing white-collar work. I expend twice as many calories as he does. Why should he have such a big house, and I'm living in a dump?" If you allow yourself to think this way, you'll stay in both the figurative box that limits your thinking and the literal box that is your house.

What if you looked at it a different way? Your neighbor isn't much smarter than you are. There is nothing he has done that you couldn't do. If he was able to land a high-paying white-collar job, then why can't you? So instead of looking at your neighbor's house and seeing something you don't have, look at that house and see something you could have if you work hard enough.

It's not only comparisons with other people that can make you envious and resentful. You can make yourself unhappy just by being unrealistic about your own life. Dennis has an equation for this: $U = I-R$, meaning your level of unhappiness equals your image of how you think your life ought to be, minus the reality of where you're at or what's possible.

In fact, Dennis has had to confront this formula himself. When he was a young man, he imagined he would meet a girl, get married, and have four perfect children who would all sit around and discuss politics and theology at the dinner table. Instead, he got divorced. And at the dinner table, his kids wanted to talk about other stuff—sometimes sports or music that he couldn't stand. He eventually realized that if he didn't change his expectations he was going to be miserable.

When you stop measuring your accomplishments, possessions, and wealth against some imagined yardstick—whether it's your own or someone else's—you'll have a much easier time enjoying what you have. This practice will help you be grateful and, ultimately, happier.

The reward for taking responsibility for your life is freedom. If you understand that you are steering your own boat, then suddenly you realize that you get to choose your direction.

Freedom is powerful—so powerful, in fact, that many shy away from it. We crave security. The desire for security often trumps the yearning for freedom—so much so that people are willing to give up freedom for security.

The beach is the perfect metaphor for American freedom. The people who came to America searching for a better life landed on the beach. In 1620, the Pilgrims didn't show up in Nebraska; they showed up on the shore of Plymouth, Massachusetts. They jumped off the *Mayflower*, cracked a beer, threw a frisbee, and enjoyed the new land. (This account may be more metaphorical than factual, but you get the idea.) That tradition continued for centuries—from New Jersey to San Diego, beaches have always been places Americans go to unwind and let loose. In southern California, in particular, the beach epitomized the laid-back, freedom-loving culture of the prosperous post-war America.

But a few decades ago, something new started happening.

When you arrived at a beach, you used to see maybe one sign. It would say something like, "No littering," or, "No lighting vans on fire." These simple rules helped everyone get along (and they kept the third degree burns from van fires to a minimum). But go to a southern California beach now, and you immediately have multicolor bonded steel yelling at you: "No Dogs!" "No Smoking!" No Fires!" "No Alcohol!" "No Digging!" "No Sandcastles!" "No Frisbees!" It looks like a Fuddruckers menu—the signage goes on forever in a senseless blur of colors and fonts that has lost all meaning.

Each new sign is the result of someone trying to solve a problem and seeking redress from authority figures—in this case, the government. Some malcontent complains, the government creates a regulation, and a sign is put up to give notice and require compliance. Then another malcontent gets malcontented about something else. Rinse, repeat. And by the way, the government never shows up and removes signs. Once a regulation exists, it doesn't ever go away.

Just like those college campus administrators trying to please everyone and guarantee safe spaces for all, the government has tried so hard to make every beach-goer comfortable that it has become nearly impossible to have any fun. And it's all thanks to unhappy people who couldn't just go to the beach and have a good time without letting little things bother them.

Don't be one of those people.

Thankfully, the beach of life doesn't need many signs for everyone to have a great time. We were able to boil it down to eight guidelines for happiness. These aren't necessarily rules, but some things to remember to stay happy:

- You are not lucky. Your success or failure depends on your hard work.
- No one else is responsible for you.
- No one can oppress you, or lift you up, without your participation.
- Abandon the language of losers. Think and talk like someone who gets things done.
- Hard work and accomplishment get rewarded.
- Place a high value on freedom—both yours and everyone else's. It's the reward for responsibility.
- Be grateful.

This may seem like an odd way to conclude the journey through the politically correct culture. But as you've seen, the problems on college campuses are caused by people who are miserable: masochists who love the idea that they have been oppressed and that life is a dead-end for them. It may be cathartic to spout this off during a teach-in or to shout it during a protest. There may be some short-term endorphin rush that comes from banning an old white male's work from the English curriculum or getting a conservative speaker dis-invited from speaking on campus.

Yet these remain the sad actions of a sad group of people—who want you to join them in their misery.

The choice is yours.

REASON FOR HOPE

I n September 2017, University of California-Berkeley looked like a community preparing for a war. Police in riot gear erected metal barriers. Large swaths of the campus were closed off. The *East Bay Times*, a local newspaper, reported that the Berkeley City Council had voted to permit police to use pepper spray on violent demonstrators, the first time in twenty years the tactic had been permitted.[1]

Ben Shapiro was coming back to Berkeley.

After drawing national criticism when a previous speech by Shapiro had been moved to a venue with an exorbitant rental fee, U.C. Berkeley opted to waive any venue fees. On top of that, they ponied up for the extra security they thought they would need after watching

Milo Yiannopoulos's visit degrade into a riot. That had happened just 255 days before, and it had been followed by heated political rallies in the meantime. Media reports put the school's security tab for the Shapiro event at somewhere around $600,000.[2]

Student protestors demonstrated the day before the speech. Standing in front of placards and signs denouncing Donald Trump, one woman read a prepared speech from her phone. "There's no free speech for fascists," she warned. "Their words are violent, and for every action there is an equal and opposite reaction."

(The protesters might have been surprised had they bothered to do a quick Google search. Shapiro has vociferously disagreed with both President Trump and Yiannopoulos—in both cases, quite publicly. And they call this a research university?)

"There will be resistance, and it will not be peaceful… Resistance to violent hate speech is not an act of hate. It is an act of love," she continued, without irony.

Dan Mogulof, Berkeley's Assistant Vice Chancellor in charge of Executive Communications, wasn't buying it.

"The Constitution is absolutely clear," Mogulof told Dennis and Adam when they interviewed him for *No Safe Spaces*. "Particularly as a public institution, we cannot and will not discriminate against speakers because of their perspectives or because of the beliefs of those that wish to host them."

"But it's not just a matter of compliance with the law," Mogulof added. Without inviting other perspectives, he said "…. we can't meet our educational goals."

Shapiro's April 2016 speech at Berkeley, seventeen months prior to the controversial September 2017 event that made Berkeley look like the start of the Hunger Games, had been a relatively uncomplicated event that came and went with little disruption. But since that simpler time, the 2016 election had helped focus left-wing organizing efforts. Antifa, a group that claims to be anti-fascist while trying to shut down viewpoints with which it disagrees, has mobilized people on and off campus to create real violence in response to the imagined violence of debate and rhetoric.

So in September of 2017, there were demonstrators rallying outside the hall where Shapiro was scheduled to speak. But he walked calmly through the building's hallways, chatting with staff and event organizers. On stage, a student presenter introduced him to "The People's Republic of Berkeley," and he bounded to the lectern.

"There are students who do want to hear differing views, who don't want to be told that they can only hear one view," Shapiro told the crowd during his speech.

After his talk, Shapiro launched into a question and answer session with a twist.

"If you disagree with me, you raise your hand, and you come to the front of the line," he told the questioners, "Because discussion makes the country better."

Mogulof was impressed. "The guy gets it," he told us. "That's what a university is supposed to be all about."

It was worth spending more than half a million dollars to make sure the event could happen without incident.

"You can't have free speech at an event that gets shut down," Mogulof told us. "We spent that money not just for safety. We spent that money for the Constitution of the United States of America."

You can count Mogulof among the folks on college campuses concerned about the values of free and open debate.

"We have our work cut out for us," he said, referring to college faculty and administrations. "There are broad societal and even parenting trends that have undermined students' understanding of... how to deal with things that we don't agree with in a civil, nonviolent manner."

(Berkeley did offer counselling services to any students who felt "threatened" by Shapiro's visit. But, hey—baby steps, right?)

$\oslash$

Picture this: a seventy-year-old Jewish man from Brooklyn shows up at Clark Atlanta University, a historically black college in Atlanta, and proceeds to debate five young black men on racial politics in America.

You would be excused for snickering to yourself or wondering if maybe the Jewish gentleman was looking to pick a fight. Then you'd learn that it's Dennis Prager, and suddenly it would make sense. (As should be obvious by now, he has a weird sense of fun.)

Over thirty minutes, the discussion ranged from white privilege to systematic racism. Dennis didn't mince words, try to use politically correct language, or sugarcoat issues. He told the gentlemen he was speaking with that he didn't believe in systemic racism, and that he thought that a young black man raised by two parents had a better shot at success than a young white man raised in a single-parent household.

These weren't easy topics, and as the six men talked things over, there were many points of disagreement. If Dennis had said some of these things in a classroom rather than on a quad, he might have been given a failing grade or been forced to answer to charges of creating a hostile environment for his fellow students. But no one got offended. There was no shouting, no finger pointing, and no one walked off in disgust. If anything, there was a palpable sense of relief among the students Dennis talked to—unlike many other white people who had spoken to them, Dennis had no qualms challenging the black students' assertions, asking them questions about their own experience, and engaging in honest debate. He didn't show up to talk down to anyone by validating victimhood.

No one left agreeing with everyone else 100 percent, but that wasn't the point.

Students thirst for engagement, discussion, and the pursuit of truth. Dennis does the same thing at every campus he visits. He spent two hours going back and forth with a classroom full of students at Kingsborough College, which is part of the City College of New York system. They talked about everything from economics to gender politics. (Dennis even did his best Jewish grandmother impersonation, trying to convince one student to marry his long-time girlfriend.) At Berkeley Dennis spent an hour debating two liberal student leaders. As he and Adam have done speaking engagements on campus together, Q&A remains an important part of each event.

The amazing thing about these engagements is that they are almost always civil. It is a 180-degree difference from the Molotov cocktail-chucking, the black-clad interlopers who invaded Berkeley, the professors bent on indoctrination over academics, and the radical feminists and cultural Marxists. It turns out that the vast majority of students are still eager to hear what other people have to say.

We have to allow these conversations to occur, and we especially need to get over the idea that words can be violent. Words are just words. They can cause violence, but they aren't violent.

Whatever issues we have in this country right now cannot be solved by sweeping disagreement under the rug. If we talk about things out in the open, we probably won't reach agreement on most things. But clarity and honesty will go a long way toward helping build a bridge.

$$\oslash$$

It took some wrangling from our No Safe Spaces team, and even some lawyers getting involved, but like Ben Shapiro at Berkeley, we overcame our logistics issues. In April 2018, California State University at Northridge finally let us hold our No Safe Spaces event.

Maybe it was because they looked through their records and saw that Adam's mom was an alum, making him a legacy case, and the Chicano Studies department threatened to occupy a campus building. We prefer to think that (a) cooler heads prevailed, and that (b) the people running colleges and universities actually do want to provide a forum for free speech, even if they don't always know how.

(Actually, come to think of it, the idea of the Chicano Studies department ditching class and marching down to occupy the administration building is pretty funny. Maybe that would have been more educational. At least it would have been more entertaining.)

Remember that when we originally tried to schedule this event, there was some concern about protesters. The campus police chief must have still been worried; before the event she asked Dennis and Adam about their general discomfort level when it came to people shouting at them, heckling them, or otherwise invading what she called their "emotional space."

It was sort of funny. Both Dennis and Adam have done call-in radio. They've been to college campuses before. Dennis infiltrated the Soviet Union. Adam did stand-up comedy. They have hecklers and ne'er-do-wells invading their "emotional space" constantly.

So they told her their discomfort level: none. People can say whatever they like to the No Safe Spaces team. That was true for that evening at CSUN, and it goes for everyone they run into on a college campus in the future, too.

Their motto? Say what's on your mind. Then, let's talk about it.

NOTES

CHAPTER FOUR:
IN WHICH WE MANSPLAIN FEMINISM
AND GENDER POLITICS

1. *Campus Sexual Assault Study*, National Institute of Justice, October 2007, https://www.ncjrs.gov/pdffiles1/nij/grants/221153.pdf.
2. *Rape and Sexual Assault Victimization among College-Age Females, 1995-2013*, Bureau of Justice Statistics of the U.S. Department of Justice, 2014, https://www.bjs.gov/pdffiles1/nij/grants/221153.pdf.

3.   National Archives and Records Administration, "Nondiscrimination
     on the Basis of Sex in Education Programs or Activities Receiving
     Federal Financial Assistance; Final Common Rule," *Federal Register*
     Vol. 65, No. 169, 2000, https://www.justice.gov/sites/default/files/crt/
     legacy/2010/12/14/t9final.pdf.

CHAPTER SIX:
ACADEMIC FAILURE

1.   *Highest Education Levels Reached by Adults in the U.S. Since 1940*,
     United States Census Bureau, 2017, http://www.census.gov/newsroom/
     press-releases/2017/cb17-51.html.

2.   Nick Anderson, "Report: Seven in Ten Students Graduate From College
     with Loans, Average Debt on the Rise," *Washington Post*, December 4,
     2013, http://www.washingtonpost.com/local/education/report-finds-
     seven-of-10-students-graduate-from-college-with-loans-average-debt-
     on-the-rise/2013/12/04/a6101140-5d1a-11e3-95c2-13623eb0e1_story.
     html?utm_term=.63b2e43595e3.

3.   Nigel Chiwaya, "These Five Charts Show How Bad the Student Loan
     Debt Situation Actually Is," *NBC News*, April 24, 2019, http://www.
     nbcnews.com/news/us-news/student-loan-statistics-2019-n997836.

4.   Sandy Baum, Jennifer Ma, Matea Pender, and Meredith Welch, "Trends
     in Student Aid, 2017," College Board, October 2017, http://trends.
     collegeboard.org/sites/default/files/2017- trends-student-aid_0.pdf, 9.

5.   "Tuition and Fees over Time," College Board, 2019, http://trends.
     collegeboard.org/college-pricing/figures-tables/tution-fees-room-board-
     over-time.

CHAPTER SEVEN:
UNSAFE SPACES

1.   Nick Corasaniti, "In Christian Stronghold, Sanders Cites Golden
      Rule," *New York Times*, September 15, 2015, A16.

CHAPTER TEN:
POLITICAL CORRECTNESS MOVES OFF-CAMPUS

1.   "The Guardian View on Taylor Swift: an Envoy for Trump's Values?"
      Guardian, November 24, 2017, http://www.theguardian.com/
      commentisfree/2017/nov/24/the-guardian-view-on-taylor-swift-an-
      envoy-for-trumps-values.
2.   Taylor Swift (@taylorswift), "I'm Writing This Post about the
      Upcoming Midterm Elections on Novermber 6th, in which I'll Be
      Voting" Instagram post, October 7, 2019, http://www.instagram.
      com/p/BopoXpYnCes/?hl=en.
3.   James Damore, "Google's Ideological Echo Chamber," *Document
      Cloud*, July 2017, http://www.Documentcloud.org/
      documents/3914586-googles-ideological-echo-chamber.html.
4.   Alex Thompson, "Twitter Is Shadow Banning Prominent Republicans
      like the RNC Chair and Trump Jr's Spokesman," *Vice,* July 25, 2018.
      http://news.vice.com/en_us/article/43paqq/twitter-is-shadow-banning-
      prominent-republicans-like-the-rnc-chair-and-trump-jrs-spokesman.

CHAPTER THIRTEEN:
WHAT CAN PARENTS DO?

1.   Genesis 4:1–8

CHAPTER FOURTEEN:
HOW EDUCATORS CAN DO BETTER

1. Everett Piper, "This is not a Daycare. It's a University!" Oklahoma Wesleyan University, November 2015, http://www.okwu.edu/blog/2015/11/this-is-not-a-day-care-its-a-university/.

2. Robert P. George and Cornel West, "Truth Seeking, Democracy, and Freedom of Thought and Expression," James Madison Program, Princeton University, last Modified March 14, 2017, http://jmp.princeton.edu/statement.

EPILOGUE

1. Tammerlin Drummond, "Berkeley Council Gives Police OK to Pepper Spray Violent Protesters," *East Bay Times* (Walnut Creek), September 12, 2017, http://www.eastbaytimes.com/2017/09/12/in-contentious-vote-berkeley-council-gives-police-ok-to-use-pepper-spray-against-violent-protesters.

2. "Shapiro Event Goes Off with Barely a Hitch," *UC Berkeley News*, September 14, 2017, http://news.berkeley.edu/2017/09/14/shapiro-event-goes-off-with-barely-a-hitch/.

INDEX

A

academia, viii, ix, 6–7, 13–17, 25, 102, 110, 179, 223–24
Access Hollywood, 56
Ahmadinejad, Mahmoud, 17, 114
Allen, Tim, 12–13, 158, 163–64, 169
American Civil Liberties Union (ACLU), 18–19, 121
Amherst College, 64–65
anti-Semitism, 39, 47, 79, 81, 83
Antifa, 116–17, 247
Attkisson, Sheryl, 182–85

B

Barnard College, 62, 114. *See also* Realm, Morgan
baseball, 69–70, 125
Beck-Peter, Tricia, 73–74
Brandt, Tyler, 110–112. *See also* University of Wisconsin
Bridges, George, 5–6. *See also* Evergreen State College
Bruce, Lenny, 157, 163–69

C

Cain and Abel, 210–11
California State University, Northridge (CSUN), 13–17, 45, 251
Callen, Bryan, 160–68
campus newspaper, 47, 113
capitalism, 72–73, 80, 86, 141–142
censorship, 20, 22, 30, 73, 122, 154, 169, 172, 222
Charlottesville, 83. *See also* University of Virginia
Chesterton, G. K., 220
Christian colleges, 228
Christmas, 67, 76, 161, 164
civil rights, 21, 141, 189
Clark Atlanta University, 248
Clinton, Hillary, 41, 116, 126, 179, 190
Cold War, 9, 86, 123
College Republicans, 22, 112–18
Columbia University, 16–17, 39, 113–15
comedy, 10–11, 157–65, 168–73
communism, 222. *See also* communist
communist, 9, 86–87, 123, 142. *See also* communism
Congress, 121–2, 171, 178, 181
Constitution, 23, 28, 72, 89, 136, 246–7
Corn, Olivia, 60, 112–19. *See also* Cornell University
Cornell University, 60, 102, 112–18. *See also* Corn, Olivia
Cuba, 86, 142, 172

D

Damore, James, 152–54. *See also* Google
Dear Colleague Letter, 65–66
Declaration of Independence, 23, 72, 139
Democratic party, 41
Dennis Prager Show, viii, 9
Department of Education, 64–66, 101
Department of Justice, 54
Dershowitz, Alan, 26, 71, 80–84
Dewey, John, 224
DiAngelo, Robin, 69–71
Dillon, Kassy, 61–63, 115–16. *See also* Mount Holyoke College
diversity, 3, 36, 45, 49, 75, 108, 127, 153–54, 187
Duke University, 64

E

E Pluribus Unum, 136, 143
equality, 48, 50, 72, 137–39, 143, 149, 162
Evergreen State College, 1–6. *See also* Bridges, George; Weinstein, Bret

F

failure, 138, 141–43, 196, 198–201, 238, 243,
feminists, 58–61, 67–68, 73, 91, 249
First Amendment, 13, 18, 24, 28–29
Flagler College, 73–74
Foundation for Individual Rights in Education (FIRE), 18–20, 23,

27–31, 128, 148. *See also* Lukianoff, Greg
founding fathers, 127, 136, 144
freedom of speech, 23, 27, 29, 72, 82,
121, 187
Freud, Sigmund, 209–10

G

gay rights, 29, 38, 46, 50, 149–52,
166, 187. *See also Obergefell v.
Hodges*
gender identity, 77, 216
George, Robert, 221–3. *See also*
Princeton University
Gingrich, Newt, 113, 190
Goldstein, Michael, 108–10. *See also*
Kingsborough Community College
Google, 145, 152–55, 200, 246. *See
also* Damore, James
gratitude, 240

H

Harvard University, 25–26, 101
Hobby Lobby, 150–151

I

ID, 42–43
identity politics, 6, 37–38, 49–52, 59,
70, 87, 92, 183, 187, 195, 219
Imago Dei, 225
In God We Trust, 77, 136, 139, 143
Intercollegiate Studies Institute, 90
intersectionality, 80–82, 100

J

Jandhyala, Pranav, 22–23, 117. *See
also* University of California, Berke-
ley
Japan, 33, 201
Jim Crow, 41, 43, 158
Jones, Van, 43, 189–92
Judaism, ix, 7–9, 39–40, 76, 79,
81–83, 107–8, 126, 199. *See also*
Zionists

K

Kavanaugh, Brett, 184–85
Kimmel, Jimmy, 11, 18, 158, 223
King, Jr., Martin Luther, 48, 50, 187
Kingsborough Community College
108–9, 249. *See also* Michael Gold-
stein

L

lawsuit, 153, 191
liberalism, 51, 71–73, 80–4
liberty, 25, 136–39, 143, 225
Lorde, Audre, 90–91
Loveline, 11, 16
Lukianoff, Greg, 18–21, 23–24,
27–31, 71, 128, 148. *See also* FIRE

M

mansplaining, 59,
Marranos, 107–8, 118
Marx, Karl, 86–87. *See also* Marxism
Marxism, 89, 94, 98, 249. *See also*
Marx, Karl

microaggression, 77–78, 140
Mogulof, Dan, 246–47
Molotov cocktail, 22, 131, 249
Mount Holyoke College, 61–63, 115–
  16. *See also* Dillon, Kassy

N

Nazi, 46, 170, 180–81, 219
New York Times, 8, 37, 83, 115, 154
No Safe Spaces tour, 17, 34, 46, 60,
  88, 159, 205
North Hollywood, California, vii, 10,
  34–35, 233

O

Obama, Barack, 43, 48, 64, 98, 101,
  131, 178, 180, 185, 189
Obergefell v. Hodges, 149. *See also* gay
  rights
Oklahoma Wesleyan University, 217–19,
  224–29. *See also* Piper, Everett
oppression, 38, 41–43, 77, 93, 131,
  143

P

patriarchy, 59, 127
Pell grants, 92, 233
Pepperdine University, 98
Peterson, Jordan, 85–87, 92, 95, 193,
  206–11
Phillips, Jack, 187
Piper, Everett, 218–19, 224–29. *See
  also* Oklahoma Wesleyan Univer-
  sity

police, 22–23, 45, 66, 81, 169, 245;
  campus police, 2, 5–6, 74, 250
political correctness, 6, 19, 59, 115,
  127, 129, 145, 158–59, 169, 218
Prager University (PragerU), 10, 145–48,
  154
Princeton University, 221. *See also*
  George, Robert; West, Cornel
privilege, white, 33–38, 43, 45, 48, 58,
  96, 138, 248
protests, 2–6, 16–17, 22–23, 29, 74,
  98, 110, 113–15, 121, 130, 150,
  180, 226, 234, 244, 246, 250

R

race, 1, 33, 36–38, 42–48, 58, 71, 79,
  93, 104, 135, 178, 187, 202, 215
rape, 54–56, 65
Realm, Morgan, 114–16. *See also* Bar-
  nard College
Rickey, Branch, 70
Robinson, Jackie, 69–71
Robinson, Tommy, 114, 116
Rubin, Dave, 49–52, 71, 175, 181,
  186–88

S

safe spaces, 6, 13, 17, 21, 24, 80-81,
  103, 108, 117, 127, 139, 144, 148,
  224, 243
Sanders, Bernie, 3, 115
Santorum, Rick, 112-13
Schulz, Andrew, 169
Security, 16-17, 23, 95-96, 112-14,
  164, 241-42, 245-46

self-esteem, 41, 45, 216, 239
sexual assault, 54-58, 64-65, 68, 185
Shakespeare, William, 90
Shapiro, Ben, 23, 115, 121, 130, 245, 250
Sheehan, Colleen, 102. *See also* Villanova University
Slavery, 40, 44, 111, 136, 141
"Sleepwalker", 53-54
smoking, 167-68, 239, 242
social justice, 3, 27, 72-73, 77, 109, 111, 150-51, 159
social media, 127, 147-48, 151, 176, 188, 234
Soviet Union, 9, 85-87, 123
Sports, 11, 39, 63, 125, 127, 198-201, 241
Stanford University, 40
Steele, Shelby, 40, 44, 48
Supreme Court, 64, 89, 149-50, 184, 187-88

T

The Adam Carolla Show, 11
Title IX, 63, 66, 184
Tolerance, 49, 51, 56, 108, 115, 217-18
toxic masculinity, 58-59, 96, 193
trigger warning, 6, 21, 127, 144, 158, 217
Trump, Donald, 42, 56, 116, 179, 190, 246
truth, 10, 47, 59, 64, 70, 78-80, 89, 104, 157, 202, 217-20, 223, 226, 236, 249,
tuition, 96-98, 101

U

University of California-Santa Barbara, 47
University of California, Berkeley, 117, 130, 245. *See also* Jandhyala, Pranav
University of Pennsylvania, 19, 90
University of Virginia, 64
University of Wisconsin, 26, 110. *See also* Brandt, Tyler
University of Wyoming, 47

V

victim mentality, 38, 41
victimhood, 33, 38-39, 41, 43, 46, 92, 138, 187, 235, 249,
Villanova University, 102. *See also* Sheehan, Colleen
violence, 117–18, 130–31, 166, 172–73, 180, 247, 249

W

Weinstein, Bret, 1-4, 71. *See also* Evergreen State College
Welfare, vii, 34, 41, 123, 178-79
Wellesley College
West, Cornel, 221. *See also* Princeton University
Winfrey, Oprah, 78

Y

Yiannopoulos, Milo, 22, 246
Young America's Foundation, 113

Youtube, 145-48, 153-54, 158, 176, 207

Z

Zionists, 80-81